HOW TO RESTORE

# Body Decoration, Brightwork & Instruments

OSPREY
RESTORATION
GUIDE 11

# HOW TO RESTORE

# Body Decoration, Brightwork & Instruments

## Peter Wallage

Published in 1987 by Osprey Publishing Limited
27A Floral Street, London WC2E 9DP
Member company of the George Philip Group

Sole distributors for the USA

Osceola, Wisconsin 54020, USA

British Library Cataloguing in Publication Data

Wallage, Peter
    How to restore body decoration, brightwork and instruments.—
(Osprey restoration guide; 11)
    1. Automobiles—Bodies—Maintenance and repair
    I. Title
    629.2'6'0288    TL255
ISBN 0-85045-716-5

Editor Tony Thacker
Associate Editor Graham Robson

Filmset by Tameside Filmsetting Ltd, Ashton-under-Lyne,
Lancashire
Printed in Great Britain

# CONTENTS

# Introduction

Too often, when people are looking at a car with a view to buying it for restoration, they take note of the major items which need attention such as the mechanics, interior and bodywork, but tend to forget much of the rest. Yet it is the rest, the brightwork, the instruments, the door furniture and so on, which can often put the restoration costs of a car way beyond the original estimate and which can completely spoil the job if they are not right. . . .

In some cases there is nothing you can do but to seek professional help. Chrome-plating which has started to flake, or complex instruments, such as the older chronometric speedometers and rev counters, cannot be restored in a home workshop. Having said this, there is much in the way of component restoration which anyone with a reasonable facility for handling tools can tackle quite happily at home provided they know how.

Gleaming chrome-plate sets off the immaculate paintwork on this beautifully restored early post-war Jensen

It is my intention that this book will give you the know-how to restore many of those items which can sometimes be difficult to find for an older car but which make all the difference to the finished restoration. Instruments are a good case in point, as you are unlikely to be able to buy a new instrument over the counter for a car more than ten years old. Yet the auxiliary instruments, in particular, often kept the same internal design for years with only a change of dial and possibly grouping for different models. It is perfectly feasible in many cases to swap the insides of instruments around to put a working mechanism behind your dial.

As well as saving you money on these 'minor' restoration jobs, my aim has been to show you how, with possible adaptation as well as restoration, you can avoid what could in many cases be a long-drawn and frustrating search to replace a missing or non-working part.

Almost no special tools are needed for this work, indeed much of it can be carried out with a normal handtool kit working on the kitchen table. There is nothing mysterious about instruments, door locks and window regulators, and though many of these components appear to be 'sealed for life', someone assembled them so that someone else can take them apart. You may have to use parts from several components when rebuilding, and replace rivets with small nuts and bolts or make other adaptations, but except for a few very cheap switches and the like, most items on a car can be restored.

Other books in this series have covered the major items. Here I am dealing with the minor items which put the finishing touches to a restoration.

Peter Wallage
September 1986

# Chapter 1 | Chrome-plating

**If the plating is in good condition, last-minute polishing before the judging at a concours need take only a few minutes**

Poor brightwork gives a car a dowdy look that no amount of gleaming paintwork or smart interior can offset. All enthusiasts realize this but, in my experience of talking to entrants in club concours and rallies, many don't realize that it is often possible to do something about dull chrome-plating or stainless steel without spending a great deal of money on it.

Where the chrome-plating is flaking, or has been rubbed away by someone using harsh cleaners, there is no answer except to have the part replated, or to look around for a replacement second-hand component in better condition. But in many cases you can make the car look considerably smarter by expending more elbow-grease than money. Even when a replacement item is the only answer there are ways in which you can save quite a lot of money, once you have established a good relationship with your local plating works.

First, though, we'll have a look at what can be done without having the parts replated. Chromium is a very tough metal, as well as being highly decorative, but despite its toughness it is not waterproof. Indeed, by comparison with some other metals it is quite porous. Chrome-plating depends for its long-lasting qualities on the materials underneath it. The brown look which you often see on plating, and the thousands of tiny pin-pricks which make

Where the plating has deteriorated badly, as on this Austin A30 front grille, replating or searching for a better example at an autojumble is the only answer

**Start cleaning the chromium with the mildest of proprietary cleaners and then, if necessary, progress gradually through the harsher cleaners before deciding that you have to resort to replating**

chrome-plating look dowdy and which are quite difficult to get out with ordinary chromium cleaners, are caused by corrosion from underneath which is working its way through the porous skin of the chrome-plating itself.

Even the best chrome-plating on expensive cars is less than paper thin, and if you attack it with harsh abrasives it is only too easy to cut right through it. Start your cleaning with the mildest of cleaners, and if this does not complete the job, start working your way through the harsher cleaners until either you find one which will bring the plating up shining again, or you come to the conclusion that things have gone so far that replating or replacement is the only answer.

Where the surface of the chrome-plating is only mildly discoloured, most of the proprietary cleaners will restore it to a proper shine again, but many people who have chrome-plating that begins to look a little dowdy have tried these without much success, particularly on the worst parts. The next stage, therefore, is for you to try one of the colour-restoring polishes which are intended for paintwork—such as T-Cut or Color-Bak. When using these I have found that they tend, on chrome-plating at least, to thicken and drag quite quickly. It seems to help matters along if you add just one or two drops of washing-up liquid. This emulsifies with the cleaner and, as well as making rubbing a lot easier, it helps to lift out the grime.

The better colour-restoring cleaners do not contain abrasives. They act chemically rather than by abrasion, and though they have more effect on poor chrome-plating than proprietary chromium cleaners, they will not tackle more deep-seated corrosion. So, if you do not have any success using these, try using a good old-fashioned metal polish such as Bluebell or Brasso. These do have a slight abrasive action, enough to cut through the tough skin which protects the chromium metal itself.

It is a common misunderstanding that chromium resists corrosion and tarnishing because it is inert to the oxides and other corrosive elements in the atmosphere. In fact, the opposite is the case. Chromium is *very* reactive. So much so, that the oxygen in the air very quickly forms a

**As a last resort try a buffing wheel in your electric drill. Once again, start with the mildest of buffing soaps and gradually work your way through to the coarser ones**

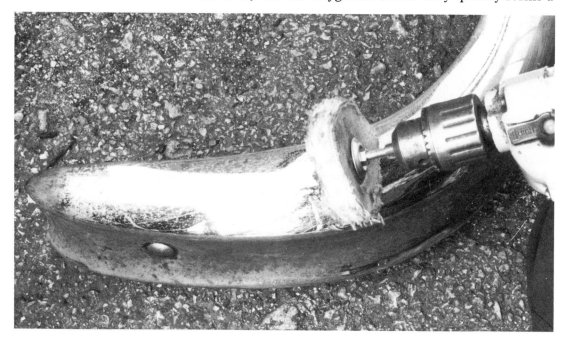

skin of tough colourless oxide which protects the metal from further attack. However, if corrosion is starting to come through the porous chromium from underneath, the discolouration will be under this tough oxide skin, which is why you sometimes need a slightly abrasive cleaner to get down through this skin and remove it. Once again, if the metal polish starts to thicken and drag as it cuts through the oxide film, try adding a drop or two of washing-up liquid.

So far, you won't have used anything that will cut through the chrome-plating with one application (unless you rub for hours and hours), though continuous cleaning with metal polish will go through it, given time. However, metal polish is not all that effective against that dull grey look which afflicts some chrome-plating, and which often shows up as a network of thousands of tiny lines like cobwebs under that oxide skin. This is because the actual surface of the chromium has lost its polish, as well as discolouration due to corrosion coming through from underneath. The only way to get rid of this without having the part replated is to repolish the surface of the chromium, and for this you will need something which acts a little faster than metal polish and a rag.

If you fit a rag buffing wheel to your electric drill, you will get a much faster polishing action than when rubbing by hand, so try this with metal polish first, to see if that will do the trick. If it does not, you will then need to acquire two or three grades of buffing soap. Buffing soap looks and feels a little like hard ordinary soap, but it contains a finely-ground abrasive. It comes in sticks or blocks, and these are graded from fine to coarse usually, though not always, by colour. The red-coloured buffing soaps are usually the mildest, and from these you can work up through dark brown and yellow, to grey—which has so coarse a cutting action that you have to be very careful how you use it. It is so coarse in its action that on a large-diameter, high-speed buffing wheel it is used to buff out the casting marks and surface imperfections on aluminium castings to bring them up to a smooth and shiny finish. You can imagine what it will do with thin chrome-plating if you use it too energetically.

You often see buffing soap on sale in DIY shops, but you

It is not worthwhile trying to do much with hub caps which have deteriorated to this state. Hub caps in much better condition can be found at a fraction of what it would cost to replate the old ones

will get a better selection of grades in a tool shop which caters for the engineering trades. Milder even than the finest buffing soap usually stocked by engineering tool shops (though most will get it for you if you order it) is a deep red material known as jeweller's rouge. As its name suggests, this is used for polishing silver and jewellery. It is ideal for a final polish on chrome-plating which has developed that cobweb-look over the surface.

Once again, start with the mildest buffing soap you can find, and work through to the coarser ones *only as a last resort*, for you might soon come to the point of no return where you find that your work is actually taking the chrome-plating right off the metal. If this happens, then the only answer is to stop and have the part replated. But if it should happen, at least you know that you have tried with the mildest ones, and if these did not bring the chrome-plating back up to a nice glittering finish, you are really no worse off than when you started.

You may well find that although you have been successful in cleaning chrome-plating in this way, the nice bright finish does not last and that you soon see pin-pricks of discolouration showing up again. All you have done is to remove the symptoms, but not cured the cause. Underneath top-quality chrome-plating there should be a layer of nickel-plating and underneath that, in the very best process, there should be a layer of copper, before you find the steel base. The yellowish look which you sometimes find on dowdy chrome-plating is due to the normal oxidation of nickel underneath the chromium which is coming through, but when you start getting deep brown and red stains coming through, this means that the nickel and copper coatings have begun to give way, and that the steel underneath is starting to rust. So, if you want to stop the rust coming through again, this must be treated with a rust killer.

New sidelamps like these are still available, and though they are quite expensive they cost less than having the old ones replated

Most plated trim strips are held to the body by spring clips which are either riveted, or pushed into pre-drilled holes. They are a regular place for rust to start underneath the trim

The only way to get at this rust is through the pin-pricks where the rust erupted. Because chromium oxidizes very quickly, you have to use a rust killer almost immediately after cleaning off the chromium oxide film. If you leave it even until the next day, the oxide film which has formed during that time will stop quite a lot of the rust killer from reaching the steel.

Almost any good-quality rust killer will do the job, but the ones which leave a hard blue or black deposit on the steel after use will still leave the chrome-plating looking rather pockmarked, because instead of seeing thousands of tiny pin-pricks of brown-coloured rust, you now see thousands of tiny pin-pricks of blue-coloured converted rust. One effective way I have found of solving this problem, though there may well be other rust killers which do not dry blue or black, is to use Kurust. This is a thick grey rust-killing paint which dries to a light grey finish rather than a blue or black finish, and which dries only where it has acted chemically on the rust.

If you paint, say, a bumper with Kurust after you have polished and washed it down with a spot of white spirit, the Kurust will stay more or less tacky on the surface, though it will eventually dry. If you leave it for 24 hours—by which time it should have done its job on the steel under the chromium—and then wipe over the surface with methylated spirit, the Kurust which has not been in contact with rusty steel will then wash away. In the tiny pin-pricks where it has reacted with the steel you will be left with a lightish grey deposit which, though it might take the final edge off the shine of chromium, is at least preferable to rust-coloured pin-pricks, and which will resist further attacks by rust for a surprisingly long time.

Finally, if you finish off with a good old-fashioned hard wax such as the original Simoniz, you will then finish up with chrome-plating which stays smarter, longer.

If all your cleaning efforts prove unsuccessful, and you have, finally, to resort to having the parts replated, you can still save yourself quite a lot of money provided you find a co-operative plater. If you can reduce the amount of work the plater has to do, then he should charge you less than if you just unbolt, say, a bumper and dump it on his counter

This nylon button clip for a trim strip will not rust and can be located in the strip before it is pushed into position on the body

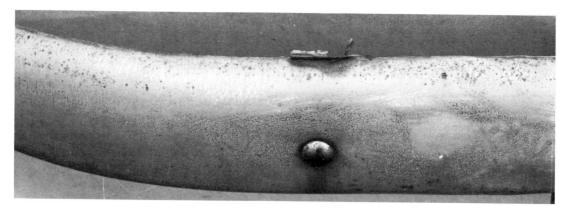

The plating on this bumper did not look too bad, but closer inspection showed that it was flaking and peeling. No amount of cleaning will restore these flaked areas

complete with overriders and various odd steel brackets still hanging on to the back of it. Do check with him first, though, as one or two platers to whom I have spoken have a standard list of charges which allows for people dumping parts on the counter, though not with other bits hanging on them, at least in a condition which needs a considerable amount of work before they can even be put into the cleaning bath. These platers work according to a 'menu-pricing' philosophy, reasoning that they are going to get some parts which want more work than others, but the standard charge (if it is pitched about halfway between the best and the worst cases) will eventually even things out.

Before you take the parts along, check with your plater to find out what sort of quote he will give you if you deliver the parts completely dismantled and in a clean condition where they can go straight into his chemical cleaning bath. No plater will dump rusty, oily parts into his cleaning bath, because these form sludge at the bottom of the tank which eventually has to be cleaned out. He will employ somebody, usually an unskilled worker, to clean the parts up to a reasonable condition before they go along to the chemical cleaning bath. You will pay for this labour time, and unfortunately, because it is unskilled labour, you find only too often that the person doing the work has a rather casual 'bash-and-hope' mentality, and it is not unknown for parts which are perhaps a little difficult to get apart to be damaged in the process. You will always find a notice somewhere at the plater's workshop, or in his agreement,

Don't send your parts to the plater without completely dismantling them. He will charge you more for taking things apart, and will not accept responsibility should he shear off any rusted studs

that he can accept no responsibility for parts which are damaged because of seized nuts or other reasons which are not just pure negligence on the part of his employees.

If you make friends with your plater, he will tell you how much cleaning up the parts will save you money. He will also be able to tell you whether or not he has the facilities for taking out the odd dent or twist and how much this is likely to cost. Obviously he cannot quote for straightening, say, a badly bent bumper or a badly dented headlamp shell without seeing it, but at least you will know whether or not he will undertake such work. Some platers have facilities for this, some have not. Those who have not, usually send the parts out to another local engineering firm which has rolling and pressing machines to do the job. Most of these firms have no retail counter and deal with the trade only, and though some platers will insist on handling this sort of work themselves, a few will give you a recommendation to go round to such a company with your parts direct,

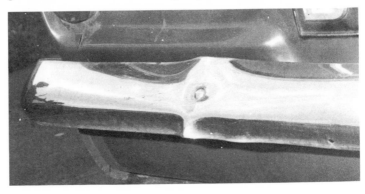

If a bumper has been distorted like this one, don't attempt to beat out the disfiguration. You will probably make it worse because the metal is stretched, and the plater will charge you correspondingly more to roll it flat again

mentioning the plating firm's name. In this way, you may get a cheaper quote than the plater would have to charge you, bearing in mind that his profit margin has to be taken into account plus, again, the labour time for someone to take your parts round and then go and collect them again.

When it comes to deciding whether or not a part is worth straightening or having dents taken out, or whether it is more economical to look for a second-hand part in better condition, there are no easy recommendations. Sometimes, what might look like major damage can be rolled or pressed out relatively easily. In other cases, what appears to be minor damage might present a major, and expensive, problem to the man who is repairing it. Most of these problems arise where the metal has been stretched, or where a thin steel pressing—such as a radiator shell or headlamp shell—has corroded from the inside to the point where, when it is thoroughly cleaned and degreased, there are tiny pepper-pot holes through the base material itself. A component which is like this is almost past reclaiming, unless it is a particularly rare component from a vintage or veteran car, where no new components exist, and even then the cost of restoration is likely to prove very high. Some platers will undertake major repair work of this nature, or know somebody who will do it, but others will not touch it. On one point, though, all the platers with whom I have discussed this were in agreement. Do not attempt to beat out any dents yourself. Amateur panel beating or straightening very often puts further damage into the component which makes it much more expensive, and in a few cases even impossible, to repair economically.

Sometimes, you may find yourself in the awkward situation where you have managed to clean the chrome-plating but are faced with a relatively minor repair. The sort of thing I have in mind here is a radiator grille on which some of the slats have become loose at one end. In some cases concerning quite elaborate radiator grilles which are made up from thin steel or sometimes brass pressings, the parts were originally plated and polished before they were put together because of the difficulty of polishing the surface of the chrome-plating after the parts were assembled. In instances such as these, you often find

Top right **Radiator badges suffer from being grit-blasted at the front of the car. If they are plastic with incised letters, like this Wolseley badge, they can be restored quite easily at home, but if they are enamelled you will have to find a specialist to restore them**

Bottom right **Taking apart a radiator like this only means drilling out the old rivets, and they can be easily replaced after repair by a home blind-riveting tool**

that the slats are soft-soldered into place. Hard-soldering or brazing would have been much stronger, but the heat of this process would then have destroyed some of the chrome-plating. You will sometimes find that instead of soft solder, the parts are held in place by a rivet or a single, quite small, spot-weld where the localized heat has not spread enough to damage the plating. Here you are faced with three choices. You can either soft solder the part back into position, you can rivet it or you might even use a glassfibre resin to hold it.

If you choose to soft solder it, you are likely to run into all sorts of difficulties if you try to use a soldering iron (even a large one), and you will end up with an unsightly fillet of solder down the edge of the join. The only way to tackle this sort of thing is with a small flame. Something like a butane gas torch, on which you can turn down the flame until it is about the same size as a large flame on a gas

Where you have to resort to soldering as a repair, use resin-cored solder and the smallest flame you can coax from a blowlamp. If you need extra flux use a non-corrosive paste flux, but never use killed spirits

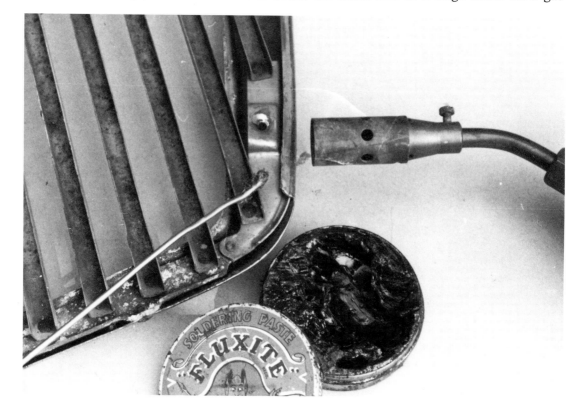

cigarette lighter, will do the job quite nicely. The way to set about it is first to clean thoroughly the two surfaces you want to solder, and then to coat both of them with a thin layer of solder. You then need to clamp them together, apply the heat from the flame until the solder runs together, and finally leave them to cool off. The best solder to use for this type of work is a resin-cored solder of the type sold for electrical and electronic work. The resin flux in these solders is non-corrosive, and all you need to do afterwards is merely give the part a wash off in warm water.

If you are dealing with a fairly large area, more than about half an inch square, it is probably advisable to put some extra flux on the surfaces you have tinned with solder *before* you clamp them together. Choose a brown paste flux, such as Fluxite, and make sure that this is non-corrosive (the description on the outside of the tin will make this quite clear). Avoid using a liquid flux, such as Bakers Fluid, which is usually made from hydrochloric acid 'killed' with zinc. These liquid fluxes are very effective, but they are also highly corrosive, and even with extensive washing off afterwards, you are likely to find green corrosion growing out from the joint within a few weeks. The surface of the chrome-plating will probably have discoloured slightly from the heat of your flame, but usually this is quite light, often a brown or blue colour, and may be removed, either with metal polish or with one of the proprietary 'blue removers' which you can get from a motorcycle repair shop, where it is sold for taking the blue discolouration off the front part of chrome-plated exhaust pipes.

Now we come to the absolute bugbear of chrome-plated parts and trim on cars, which are the die-cast parts that are made from Mazak. This is an alloy based on magnesium, aluminium and zinc, which casts into beautifully sharp contours but which, when it gets a little old, tends to erupt in blisters and small pimples. Some platers will tell you that they cannot do anything about a Mazak component which has deteriorated like this. Others might offer to have a go at a repair but will not guarantee what the part will look like afterwards, because it will have to be buffed down so much, and you are likely to lose the definition of raised

Pitting and pimpling on die-casting is the bugbear of restoring brightwork on a car. Some platers will take on the job but others will decline to handle this material

outlines on such things as badge motifs and nameplates. In any case, most platers will tell you that they cannot guarantee how long the replated part will retain its new plating.

Is there no way round this problem? Yes, it appears that there is, provided you can get the co-operation of a friendly plater, because the successful method uses a process which does not normally come within the services he offers. I first read of this method in an American magazine, and though I have not actually tried it myself, I have spoken to one or two people who have tried it and who tell me that it has worked, though at that time there had not been sufficient time to check on its lasting qualities.

The first thing to do is to work over the surface of the blistered Mazak part with fairly coarse buffing soap on a rag buff, plus some very fine wet-and-dry rubbing-down paper, until the surface is absolutely smooth again. This will take quite a lot of the plating off, but that does not matter. Next we come to the work which takes ages and ages to complete, and on the thoroughness of which success depends. The time it takes and the, probably at best, only 90 per cent chance of success is why most platers will not tackle it themselves. You find that where blisters have appeared in the chrome-plating, there are actually small craters of corrosion underneath in the Mazak material itself. You need to work over all these little pockmarks or craters, each one individually, picking them out either with a very tiny drill, a sharp pointer or, better still, a dentist's burr with which he drills teeth. If you have a word with your local dentist he will usually be able to supply you with plenty of used ones which are quite suitable for what you want. For your needs, mount them in a flexible drive run from your power drill and run your drill at the slowest possible speed. The slow speed of the normal two-speed power drill is far too fast, so you will need some

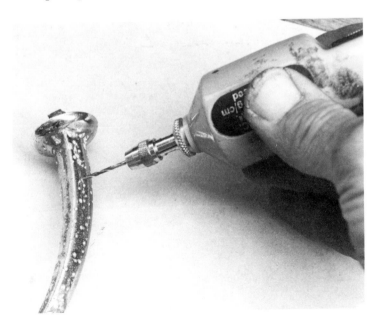

If a pitted die-casting is irreplaceable and you can find a co-operative plater, you can sometimes work with him by doing a lot of the work yourself. The first step is to drill out all the corrosion from the pitted holes. A mini-drill such as this is most useful

Right **After the plater has
chemically cleaned the drilled
casting you can fill the drilled-
out pitmarks with soft solder**

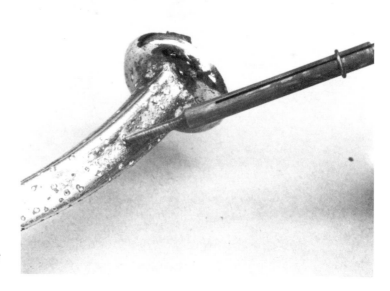

Below **As an alternative to soft
solder on small pitting you can
fill it by rubbing with a block of
annealed soft copper**

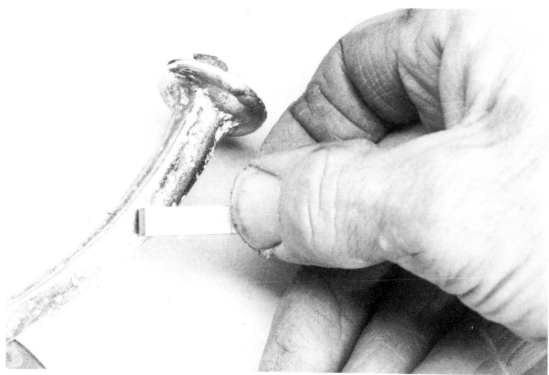

sort of electronic regulator in the powerline to the drill to slow it down.

The reason you have to pick out these pockmarks individually to get rid of the corrosion is that just about any chemical which will lift the corrosion out of these craters will also attack the Mazak itself, and by using such compounds you finish up with something looking like a well-licked lollipop rather than a sharply die-cast component. When you have been over all the pockmarks, it is time to take the part to the plater and ask him to put it in his chemical cleaning bath. Then when you get it back, take it home and either fill up the pockmarks with soft solder, which can be done without melting the Mazak *if you are careful* using a small electric soldering iron and resin-cored solder, or if the pockmarks are not too deep, rub them over with an annealed piece of soft copper until they have all been filled in. To anneal copper to make it soft, use the opposite way to annealing steel. Bring the copper up to a nice bright cherry-red colour and then quench it immediately in cold water.

When the pockmarks are filled, lightly buff over again with a fine buffing soap and a fairly slow speed on the buffing mop, and then take the part back to the plater. He will then put it into a cleaning bath which will not attack the soft solder, but which will get rid of your dirty fingermarks and any oxidation on the surface, and from there he will transfer it straight to the plating vats where he will plate it first with copper, then with nickel and finally with chromium.

Even though you have personally done a lot of the preparation work, this is quite an expensive business, and only worth doing on Mazak parts for which you cannot get an unblemished replacement. As I said, not all platers will do this work. Many of them just want straightforward commercial work. But if you can find a small plater who will take an interest in what you are doing, and is willing to experiment with you on the basis that you are setting out the job so that all responsibility for the final finish must rest with you and not with him, it is a way of getting over the problem.

# Chapter 2 | Door and ignition locks

Closely allied to the problems of Mazak door handles is the problem of the door locks. It can be frustrating to search, at a breaker's yard or an autojumble, for a locking handle for your door or boot with the chrome-plating in better condition than your original one, only to realize that the law of the cussedness of inanimate objects invariably dictates that the only one you can find in perfect condition lacks a key. It can be more than frustrating, indeed it can be thoroughly annoying, to buy a car (as I have on several occasions) and be handed only one key—for the ignition. The key which locks the doors and the boot is missing and, of course, the ignition key does not fit them.

With older cars, where the key number was stamped on the outside of the lock for all to see, you stood a reasonable chance of getting a replacement key. But then so did anyone else—including a thief—who wanted to get in. With later anonymous, bland-faced locks you can try for hours with a huge box of keys to find a match and still not come up with the right one. You *might* be lucky enough to be able to buy new lock barrels for your handles—complete, of course, with new keys. You might even be very fortunate when you take out the old lock barrels to find the key number stamped on the barrel, though this is relatively unusual. However, with older cars the chances are that when you go into the main dealer, the storekeeper will suck his teeth, shake his head and say: 'Sorry, we haven't had one of those in for years.'

There is an answer. Instead of searching for a key to fit the lock you have, alter the lock to fit the key you've got. In some cases this job is very simple, but in others it is a little more time-consuming, although still reasonably easy.

If you get a lock without a key you can try for hours and hours with bundles of keys without finding one which will work

Car keys are coded by letters and numbers. The letters refer to the series and the numbers to a particular lock

Even the worst case, where you find the handle you want but it is in the locked position, can be tackled with a little ingenuity, patience and fiddling.

For many years most British cars have been fitted with Wilmot Breeden locks, the ones with the word 'Union' on the key, but almost all other barrel locks are built on the same principle. Mounted in the barrel of the lock are a number of spring-loaded plates, or tumblers as they are usually called, even though in this case they do not tumble. When the key is not in the lock, the springs push the

Keys in the same series have the
same grooves so they will fit any
lock of that series, but they will
only turn if the serrations, coded
by the figures, are right for that
particular lock

tumblers out from the side of the barrel. With the barrel in
the locked or unlocked position, these poke out and engage
in slots in the barrel sleeve so the barrel will not turn. When
the key is pushed in, the serrations along the key move the
tumblers so that their ends are flush with the barrel, thus
allowing it to be turned. It is the serrations which line the
tumblers level with the barrel. The slots in the side of the
key engage in a castellated key-way at the front of the barrel
which is put there to locate the key and deter anyone
from poking in a screwdriver, penknife blade or a piece of
wire to try to line up the tumblers.

Keys come in various series. Some of the Wilmot
Breeden series are FA, FS, FD, FP, MRN and so on. All
the keys in the same series have the same slots cut along the
sides of them. Each key also has a number which denotes

the shape of the serrations along its edge. So, for example, any FS key will slide into any FS series lock. But it will line the tumblers flush with the barrel and turn it only if the serrations are cut to match a lock with the same number as well as the same letter series.

At this point you may be beginning to see a clue here. Instead of searching for a key of the right series and with the right serrations, you should find a key of the right series so that it fits in the barrel, and then you should alter the height of the tumblers to suit the serrations which are cut in the key you've found. The theory is quite simple—most of the serious troubles you are likely to meet are in getting the lock apart to take out the barrel, particularly with the type where the handle turns, and the handle and lock you want to take apart have been left in the locked position. Locks for the older type of separate ignition switch (before the days of steering column locks), glove compartment lid locks or usually any lock where the latch is operated by the barrel being turned, are usually much more simple, but I will describe those later. First we will have a look at the difficult ones.

On the type of lock where the whole handle turns, the end of the barrel has an eccentric pin cast on it. This pin engages with a slot cut off-centre in a small oblong steel block, so that as the barrel turns, the block moves up or down. With the barrel in the locked position, this block sticks out of the side of the handle and engages with some

**Most car barrel locks work by having an eccentric pin on the end of the barrel which moves a locking bar in and out of a slot in the housing**

fixed part of the housing so that the handle cannot be turned. When the barrel is in the unlocked position, the block is pulled back, so that its end is flush with the outside of the handle, thus allowing the handle to turn.

Unfortunately, when the block is poking out of the handle it also stops you from separating the handle from the housing, and until you separate them you cannot get at the fastening that holds the barrel in the handle. And until you get at the fastening . . . this is a very difficult problem.

Sometimes you will have to file off four small pips on the square steel shaft to get an end cover off. If you find you cannot raise more pips easily when you put it back, you can drill a hole about $\frac{1}{16}$ in. in diameter through the shaft, and then use a small split pin to hold the end cover in position. If you keep the hole small you will not weaken the shaft. The big problem is a locking block which you find in the locked position.

On a few locks it is possible to reach the protruding part of the block from the back with a hacksaw blade or even with a tiny grinding wheel in a mini-drill and cut it off. You

**On this type of lock you usually have to file down four pips on the steel shaft before the lock will come apart**

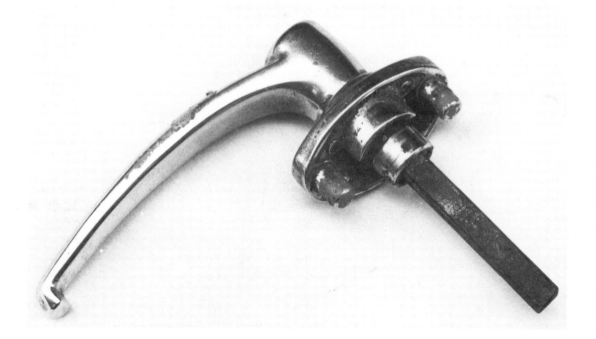

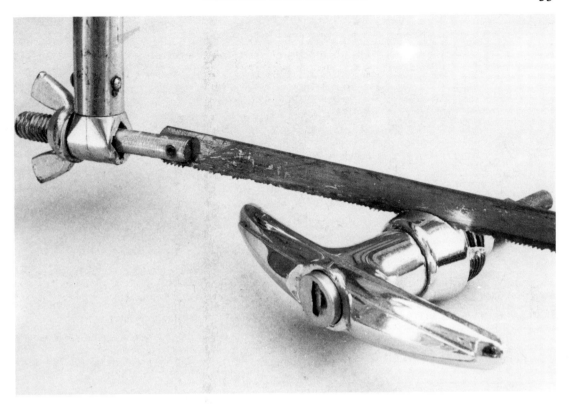

can then replace it with a block from almost any lock of the same make on which the handle turns because most of the barrel sleeves are the same diameter and the blocks are pretty well standard. Alternatively, you can modify one or file up a new block from a piece of square steel bar which should not be terribly difficult if you have a few tools and some expertise.

If cutting out the block proves to be impossible, you need two locks. First you must saw through the housing on one of them so that you can get out the handle and barrel. Then you need to saw through the handle and barrel of the other lock, just outside the housing, so that you can salvage this housing. Then, modify the barrel to fit the key, marry the two good parts together and—hey presto!—one good working lock.

When you have sawn away the fixed part of the lock, or cut off the protruding end of the block to separate the

As a last resort, you may have to obtain two identical locks at an autojumble and then saw through the housing on one, and the barrel on the other, to make up one new lock from the undamaged parts

Above **On this lock the barrel is held in by a key which can be taken out after the inner part is freed from its outer housing**

handle and the barrel from the rest of the lock, you still have to get the barrel out of the handle. Different makers use different methods to hold the barrel in the handle, and on different models of lock the same maker often uses a different method—for no apparent reason except that the lock is a different series.

As the barrel has to turn, there is almost always a groove cut round it into which the fastening fits. You will encounter various types of fastenings, such as brass pins driven through the sleeve, semi-circular keys and spring clips of all shapes. Even if the method of fastening is not apparent, rest assured it is there somewhere. When I worked on the shop floor in the early post-war years, new spare parts were very scarce, so we had to recondition, and often make, parts for almost anything. If someone had difficulty seeing how something came apart the shop foreman was fond of saying: 'Some damn fool put it together, so another damn fool ought to be able to take it apart.'

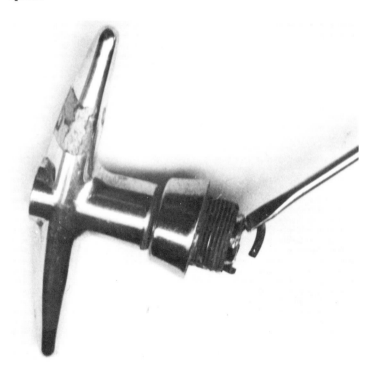

Right **On other locks the mechanism is held in the housing by a circlip at the end**

Right **As an alternative to a circlip there may be a pin driven through the end of the barrel**

Below **Many glove-box locks come apart simply by undoing a nut at the end**

There is usually no need to remove the small end cover on the barrel, but if it is damaged (as this one is) you can prise it off and then fit another one from an undamaged lock. It is usually best to glue on the cover, rather than try to swage it over

The one part of the barrel you should not try to get off is the chrome-plated end cap which is held by part of its rim being swaged over into a groove or slot at the front edge of the barrel. The only thing you could want to get at underneath is the little spring-loaded flap that is fitted to some locks to keep out the weather, but if the spring for this is broken or stuck it is no great loss, so I would advise you to leave the end cap alone. I have never known of anyone being able to take one off without distorting it and this distortion always shows when you reassemble the lock.

Earlier I said that older ignition locks (other than ignition locks with a steering lock built in them, which can sometimes be a real pain to take apart), glove compartment lid locks and most push-button door locks are usually much simpler to take apart. Where the barrel itself works the latch or the switch contacts, you can nearly always gain access from the back of the assembly.

On some ignition-switch locks, the plastic block of the switch is held to the lock by a couple of tubular rivets, and it is necessary to file the heads of these to separate the switch from the lock. This does not present any difficulty, for you can fasten the two parts together again with small screws and nuts. Be very careful, though, that when you separate the plastic block from the rest of the lock, the switch does not fly off the end of the lock. If you are not holding the switch together in a vice, it may even do this as you file off the rivet heads. There is usually a spring inside to hold the part which turns in close contact with the switch contact plates, and if the insides fly out on to the floor it can be quite a puzzle sorting out the order in which the spring, washer, insulating washer and distance piece all fit together again—always assuming that you have been able to find them all after the disaster.

Sometimes, even after you have filed the heads off the rivets, the switch may be reluctant to separate, and you may have to undo a small central nut which is sometimes locked to its shaft by solder. In some cases the solder is not very thick and will give way when you exert enough

Some ignition locks have the switch part held by a nut which is locked with soft solder. Sometimes the solder will give way quite easily when you try to undo it but in other cases you may have to soften it with a soldering iron

If you are faced with a boot lock such as this, where it seems impossible to get a screwdriver on to the two round-headed screws, try looking for circlips on the shafts. There is usually quite an easy method of removing the shafts

pressure to undo the nut. But, sometimes it will hold fast and if you turn too hard you will shear off the stud. To be on the safe side, hold a hot soldering iron against it, and if necessary put some Fluxite round it, so that the solder will run and you can undo the nut while this is still hot.

On the type of door lock which has a push-button where you push in the barrel and sleeve to open the latch, there is usually an extension of the barrel which forms the actual lock. Often this has two blocks cast on it, so that it has to be turned to a certain position to allow these blocks to pass through slots in a cover plate, thus allowing the sleeve to move. The cover plate is usually held by a couple of screws or rivets so it does not matter very much whether the barrel was left in the locked or unlocked position. In most cases the extension is quite easy to detach from the barrel, either

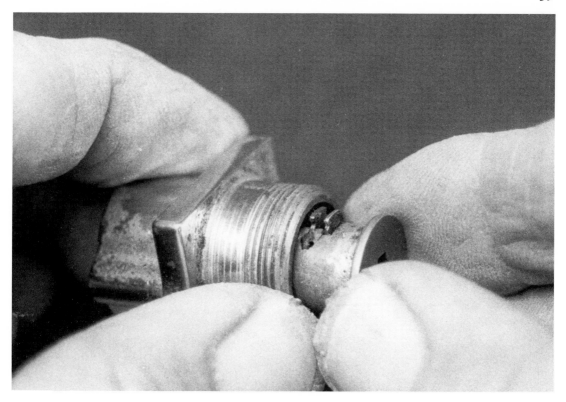

by taking off a circlip or by removing some other form of spring clip, a screw through the side or a long screw down through the middle of the extension.

You might encounter one last snag in getting the lock apart. Sometimes the slots in the handle, into which the tumblers protrude when they are in the locked position, are cut right through to the front face so that the barrel will slide out when you undo its fastening, though you may have to give the handle a tap on the bench to free it. The awkward ones are those locks in which the slots are blind at the front, so that even when you undo the fastener, the barrel will still not slide out until you put the correct key in it. Since you have not yet got the correct key, you need to poke about from the back with a small screwdriver or a thin strip of metal, and push the spring-loaded tumblers down into the barrel to let the barrel slide out. Sometimes there is not enough room to get even the smallest screwdriver in by

**You may be lucky and find that once you have freed the lock barrel it will lift straight out, even in the locked position**

In other cases the tumblers lock into a blind-ended slot so you may have to use a screwdriver or thin piece of metal to push them down while you slide the barrel out

this method, so in such a case, try with a fairly thin feeler gauge. You may possibly damage the feeler-gauge blade, but these are usually very much cheaper than locks and barrels. The whole business can be something of a fiddle, but with patience it can be done.

Now we get to the last stage, the stage you have taken all this trouble to reach. When you look at the barrel, you will see that the tumblers stick out at one side. When you put the correct series key in, the serrations will lift the tumbler plates, but because your key has not the correct serrations, the tumblers will still not line up flush with the outside of the barrel. All you have to do now is to take a fine, fairly wide file and, with the key in place, file off the ends of the tumblers that are still sticking out. If you have more than one key of the right series, choose the one which lifts at least three of the (usually) five tumblers that were sticking out before you put the key in. So long as three, or even perhaps two, tumblers pop out again when you take the key out, the barrel will still lock. When you have finished filing them flush with the barrel, take out the key again and use a very thin file or even a strip of emery-cloth between each of

the tumblers to take off the fine burr at the edge which the file will have raised.

Make sure that you get rid of all the dust and swarf from your filing operation, and put a smear of oil over things to stop the inside of the lock from corroding. The barrel is usually made of Mazak, at least on all but the older locks where, if you are lucky, the barrel might even be made of brass. Mazak in a barrel will corrode and pit just as easily as Mazak on the outside of the handle, though by being closed it may take somewhat longer to do this. If it has corroded,

Above **If you are searching for a key to modify the lock, try to find one which will take most of the tumblers down flush with the lock when it is inserted**

Top **When the key is taken out from a barrel the tumblers pop up and stop the barrel from turning in the lock**

then even if you line the tumblers up flush with the correct key, the barrel will seize so hard in the lock that you will probably break the key before you are able to turn it, so make sure you do not forget to oil it first. Oil is much better than grease for this job as it does not go hard in the cold of winter; if you do use a grease and it goes hard in the winter, the barrel will become very stiff to turn, and as the keys are usually made from a fairly soft metal there is a very good chance that you may snap off the key in the lock.

Now you have reached the point where you can put everything back together again, but please remember to make a note of the number of the key you have used—just in case you should lose it. If you do not, you will never remember it, and you will be right back at the start of this chapter once again!

# Chapter 3 | Speedometers and rev counters

I would advise against attempting to repair a speedometer head at home. This is definitely an instrument maker's job, and there are a number of specialist firms who will repair your speedo head even if this is an obsolete model. However, mechanical faults in speedometer heads are relatively rare, and in the majority of cases speedometers misbehave because of a fault in the flexible drive, or because some previous owner has been overgenerous with the lubricating of the flexible drive, particularly with oil, and some of this oil has worked its way up into the head itself. We will come to dealing with this in a moment, but first, the drive itself.

Sharp bends are the biggest enemy of flexible drives. Smiths Instruments recommend that the minimum radius for a bend in a speedometer drive cable is 6 in. (15 cm), but personally I like to keep a larger radius curve than this, if at all possible. It is most important not to have any bends close to the gearbox take-off point, nor close to the instrument head. Smiths Instruments say that the drive should come straight out of the gearbox, and the instrument itself, for at least 2 in. (5 cm), but once again try to make this straight part longer if possible.

Ranking second in the causes of flexible-drive trouble is bad support along its length, or sometimes plenty of support but in all the wrong places. The cable has to be held so that it does not wave about, but many car makers, particularly a few years ago, seemed to be quite happy with flimsy clips made from thin sheets of steel, though perhaps by no means always, with a nut and bolt or self-tapping screw to hold them in place. Sometimes these just clipped on to a convenient edge in a bodywork seam. Originally,

**Some specialist firms are making instruments specially to suit older vehicles. These examples are from Thomas Richfield and Son Limited**

most of these clips had some sort of grommet or rubber packing to protect the cable, but with the passing of the years many of these have passed away as well. Some clips have become kinked by heavy-handed owners, and even if this has not damaged the cable it may have pulled it too taut or otherwise misaligned it. Even if the rubber packing is still present, a single screw fixing for a speedometer drive clip is not a very good idea because a clip can twist around the screw and thus make the cable run in a sort of S-bend instead of running straight or in a gentle curve.

Any of these faults can make the inner cable bind in its outer casing so that instead of rotating smoothly the inner cable winds itself up and then comes free with a rush. This can make the needle waver on the dial over a range of about 10 or 15 mph so you are never quite sure what speed the car is actually doing. The needle will also waver, though it may not waver all the time, if the end of the inner cable, either at the gearbox or at the instrument head, is not engaging properly because the connectors are loose or because the outer casing has become stretched. Quite often this happens if the connector sleeve has been put on cross-threaded and has engaged with only two or three threads instead of screwing right up. There is no need to force these connector sleeves tight with pliers, though I have come across some that were so chewed and scored it seemed as though someone had been attacking them with a massive pair of pipe grips. Provided the threads are clean, finger tightness is all that is needed.

Inner cables can also stretch. To check this, disconnect the cable at the instrument end and measure the length of the inner cable protruding from the face of the flange on the outer casing. This should be about $\frac{3}{8}$ in. (9.5 mm). If it is much more than $\frac{1}{2}$ in. (13 mm) it has probably stretched.

Before you reconnect the cable, jack up one of the

**The speedometer surround on this Ford Prefect has suffered from damp getting in. A better surround from an instrument which is not working would probably be cheaper than having the original restored**

driving wheels and, with the other wheels securely chocked, run the engine at tick-over speed with the car in gear, and gently accelerate the engine. The end of the inner cable should rotate smoothly and centrally in its outer casing. If it rotates in a cone and is obviously rubbing one side of the cable, check again for sharp bends or twists in the run of the cable. But if this is not the fault, you need either a new inner cable or a complete new drive.

You can check the inner cable quite easily when it is out of the outer casing. Some inner cables just pull out from the instrument end, but some have a brass ferrule with a C-shaped washer which prevents this. If this is the case, you have to take out the washer and then extract the cable from the *gearbox* end of the drive. If you find a ferrule at the end of the inner cable with a groove for a washer, but no washer, then this could be part of the trouble.

Wipe the inner cable clean, lay it on a flat surface in a gentle curve and twist one end. It should stay flat on the surface when you twirl it between your finger and thumb. If it kicks up at one end or jumps up in the middle while it is being rotated, it needs to be renewed.

When you put back the inner cable, or when you fit a new one, smear it quite sparingly with grease. Many people make the mistake of overlubricating speedometer drives. After you have fed in the cable, pull it back up again for about 6 or 8 in. (15 or 20 cm) at the instrument end and wipe off the grease from this part. You should *never* put oil into a speedometer drive cable. The rotation of the cable will pump oil up into the instrument and possibly ruin it. Oil can also work its way up the cable into the instrument if the seal at the drive end, down by the gearbox, is missing or damaged.

The symptoms of oil in a speedometer head are that it

**If the speedometer drive is overlubricated, as here, the grease or oil will work its way up into the speedometer head**

**On most round instruments, the bezel will lift off after giving it a quarter-turn. Be careful that the glass does not drop out and break**

has sluggish operation, with possibly a slow swing of the needle back and forth right across the dial at almost any road speed. Sometimes you can get rid of the oil by washing out the instrument in petrol or benzine, but if the oil has been in there for some time and has gone hard and resembles gum more than oil, it usually means either having to send the head away to be stripped and cleaned, or finding a second-hand head which is in better condition. However, you are unlikely to damage the instrument by washing it in a suitable solvent, so if you find oil inside it is always worth having a go at cleaning it before looking for a replacement.

With some speedometers, you can take them away from behind the instrument panel and leave the glass still in place, but with others the instrument comes out from the front of the panel and has its own glass and bezel ring. In this case, the instrument is usually held in place by a metal

**Check the sealing ring under the bezel. A broken ring can allow condensation inside the instrument**

strap and a couple of nuts or thumb nuts. The bezel ring will lift off if you give it about a quarter of a turn on the fascia, but always remember to do this with the instrument upside down otherwise the glass is likely to fall out and smash. In some cases you may find that the dial is held to the casing by a couple of tiny screws at the outside edge, but in most cases the dial is held to the works of the instrument rather than to the case. The insides can usually be lifted out after undoing two, or possibly three, screws at the back of the case. It is not a good idea to try to remove the dial and pointer on a speedometer. There is a small amount of pre-tension on the pointer (given by the small

Above **On many speedometers
the movement will lift out after
undoing two, or sometimes
three, screws at the back**

Right **In many cases movements
are interchangeable. Check the
TPM figure on the dial.
Sometimes, for example, with a
rear axle ratio change, you may
have to fit a gearbox drive with
a different ratio**

hairspring which controls it), and if you do not get this amount of pre-tension correct the speedometer will not register accurately.

The best way I have found for cleaning oil out of the speedometer head is to use petrol and a small brush, something like a paintbrush from a child's paintbox. If the oil is very gummy, you may have to suspend the works in petrol for an hour or so to loosen it off. Use a jar or tin which will hold the instrument at the top without letting petrol flood all over the dial. Some dials will resist petrol quite well, but with others the petrol tends to take off some of the figures. When the petrol dries it will probably leave behind a rather mucky-looking deposit, so follow it up with a rinse in benzine, which you can get from your local chemist's shop, or give it a dose of a proprietary degreasing and cleaning fluid which you can get from a car accessory shop, usually in an aerosol can. The one my local accessory shop stocks goes under the name Ultra-Clene, but I have

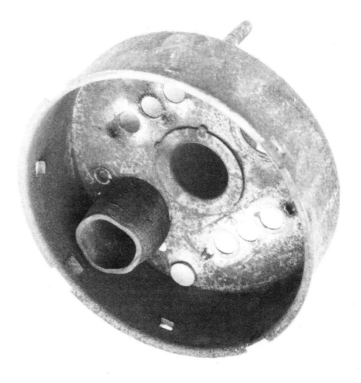

If there are warning lights inside the speedometer casing there will probably be rubber or plastic shields to direct the light towards the lens. A spot of adhesive will stop them falling out of position when you put the movement back

It is not worth trying to repair a movement in this condition, unless it is very rare. It is far easier to look for another one in better condition

no doubt there are various other suitable brands. Alternatively, you can get an aerosol of switch cleaner from your local radio or hi-fi shop. This is much the same sort of stuff and will do the job just as well. Take care to keep the cleaning spray away from the dial as it has a nasty habit of dissolving the figures on the front and, with some plastics, dissolving the face of the dial as well.

Having got rid of all the oil and left the works completely dry, you are now faced with oiling it all over again, but not, please, with engine oil, cycle oil, sewing machine oil or anything other than clock oil, which is highly refined and is formulated not to dry out—at least for quite a few years. You can get a small bottle of clock oil from your local clock repair shop, and note that there is only one correct way to apply it to the instrument. Use a small instrument or watchmaker's screwdriver with a blade of about $\frac{1}{32}$ in. diameter (not a larger electrician's screwdriver) and dip just the last $\frac{1}{4}$ in. of the blade into the oil. Then transfer the oil to the actual bearing surfaces of the instrument by just

The pointer on a speedometer is controlled by a small hairspring which also gives a slight pre-torsion when the pointer is at rest. You may have to experiment with this to get accurate readings even if the TPM number is accurate

touching the screwdriver against them. Capillary action will take the oil into the bearing where it is needed. Most people make the mistake of using too much oil. It might seem extravagant to buy a whole bottle just to use about one and a half drips in the instrument, but it is the only oil to use if you want to be successful.

If this treatment does not cure the problems, you may like to look around for a second-hand speedometer head at a breaker's yard or autojumble before you pack yours off for repair. If you do, you will need to know the turns per mile figure for your car, usually abbreviated to TPM. The speedometer from a similar car to yours may or may not have the same TPM because the axle ratio might be different or the tyres a different size. The TPM number is often marked on the dial, usually together with a code number for the instrument. The code number may be anything, but the TPM number will be a figure such as 1180 or 1251, or something of that order.

The TPM number on this dial is the one under the line, immediately above the odometer. The number in this case is 1600; the B probably denotes the ratio of the gearbox drive, though this is not always the case

If the TPM number is not marked, or if the speedometer is inaccurate and you suspect that a previous restorer may have fitted an instrument having the wrong TPM, it is quite easy to check it. Disconnect the drive from the speedometer head and push a cardboard pointer over the inner cable so that the number of turns can be counted. Then mark one of the car's driving wheels at the bottom with a chalk line and—with the gearbox in neutral—get a helper to push the car forward so that the wheel makes exactly six turns, while you count the number of turns the inner cable of the speedometer drive makes. Try to count to the nearest one-eighth of a turn. The tyres should be the correct size for the car, and they should be inflated to the pressure given in the handbook.

Now you can apply a simple formula:

$$TPM = \frac{1680 \times N}{R}$$

In this formula N is the number of turns of the inner cable for six turns of the road wheel, and R is the radius from the centre of the wheel hub to the ground, measured in inches. If you measure in centimetres, the formula becomes:

$$TPM = \frac{4233 \times N}{R}$$

The movement from a typical ribbon-type speedometer is very similar to the type with a pointer, but drives a pulley wheel

As an example, if the inner cable turns $9\frac{1}{8}$ times, and the radius R is $12\frac{1}{4}$ in., the TPM will be:

$$\frac{1680 \times 9.125}{12.25}$$

This, to the nearest whole number comes to 1251. This figure should be within 20 or 25 of the TPM number quoted on the dial of the speedometer.

There are three other types of speedometer which you may also encounter. The first is the sort in which the figures move behind a small window, the second is the older chronometric type which can be recognized by its pointer action which moves in a series of small jumps instead of a steady movement, and the horizontal ribbon-type speedometer where a red band appears in a narrow horizontal or vertical window to indicate the speed.

The first type is not really a different type of speedometer; it is the same as one with a pointer but in place of the pointer there is a disc with the numbers painted or transferred on the disc. In all other respects it is the same as the more normal type of speedometer with a pointer. The second, chronometric type, used to be very popular on sports cars and sports saloons, and is a very accurate type of instrument. However, it is most complicated inside and is costly to produce and has now been almost completely ousted by the more normal type of speedometer. If you have trouble with a chronometric type, and find that cleaning any gummy oil out of it does not make it work properly again, the best advice I can give is that you send it to a specialist repairer. The mechanism is complex and is definitely not one which will tolerate uninformed poking or fiddling.

The last type, the ribbon speedometer, has a drive mechanism very similar to that of a pointer-type speedometer, but at the end of the spindle is a small pulley around which is wrapped a length of fine nylon cord. The pulley acts rather like a windlass, and as it moves it takes with it two drum-type spools which carry the indicator ribbon. The whole set-up looks rather like the ribbons on a typewriter. The feed spool, usually the left-hand one as you look at the front of the instrument, is spring-loaded by a fairly robust hairspring underneath it. This is arranged to give the spool a small amount of pre-tension when the instrument is registering 0 mph. The right-hand, or take-up, spool has a pin, sometimes steel and sometimes plastic, on its underside. This hits against an adjustable stop to adjust the zero position. From 0 mph to maximum, the spools make just under 180 degrees rotation. The ribbon,

Instead of a pointer stop a ribbon speedometer has a stop on one of the spools and a lever under the frame. This lever can be adjusted to position the red part of the ribbon at zero

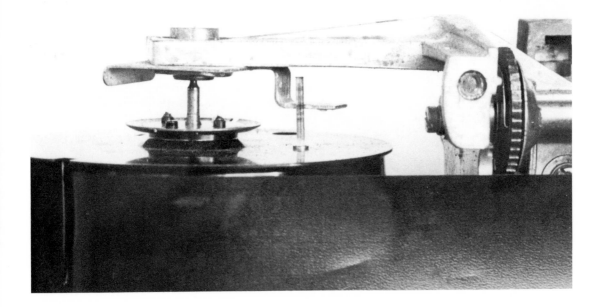

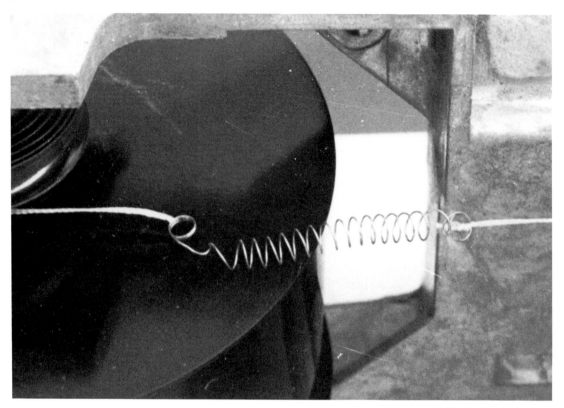

The reason for this ribbon speedometer not working was that the tension spring on the nylon cord had caught and stretched

usually made from thin flexible plastic, has loops at each end and fits on to the spools quite simply, by passing through a slot in the circumference and hooking on to a pin inside.

Fitting a replacement ribbon is not a difficult job, for you must first hook it on to the take-up spool and then wind the spool round until the pin underneath hits the back of the adjustable stop. You then wind up the feed spool by an equal amount of rotation, hook the red end of the ribbon on to it and let the hairspring coil it back. There are two adjustments. The first is the zeroing under the take-up spool, and this can be adjusted quite simply until the red part of the ribbon is opposite the o mph mark on the dial. The second adjustment is to the outer anchorage point of the hairspring which tensions the feed spool. This should not need adjusting if the replacement ribbon is the same length as the old one, and at the factory it is adjusted with the speedometer mechanism out of its case and mounted on a jig. The only way you can adjust it without this jig is to connect the mechanism to the drive cable with some sort of easily detachable pointer to indicate the position for 30 mph, and drive behind a friend's car at exactly 30 mph. If the red part of the ribbon does not coincide with the pointer the stop can be swung slightly to adjust the tension. The amount of adjustment needed for a range over, say, 5 mph is quite small so move the stop very gently, just a little at a time, if you have to do this.

Of course, it is illegal to wind back the mileage recorder on a speedometer in an attempt to make the car appear to have covered fewer miles than it actually has. However, if you fit a replacement speedometer you may want to set the mileage recorder forward on it, to the same figure as the old

The torsion of the hairspring on a ribbon speedometer is also adjustable by moving its anchor lever

one, so that the total mileage recorded for your car is accurate. Disregard any stories you may hear about being able to wind the figures back by fitting the broken end of an old speedometer inner cable into a hand drill. This does not work—all you will do if you try this is to break the mechanism. The only way to reset the figures is to take the series of drums of the mileage recorder apart and refit them to indicate the mileage you want. The method of driving the mileage-recorder drums varies sometimes between different makes and layouts of speedometer, but there is a simple mechanical drive either by a gearwheel or by a ratchet and pointer, and the method is usually self-evident when you come to examine it. To alter the figures, you have to separate the individual sections of the drum, and you will find that each one engages inside its neighbour with some form of cast-teeth or pointers, which gear each drum to the next on a 10:1 ratio. I advise that you get an old useless speedometer from a breaker's yard or autojumble and take the mileage recorder apart to see exactly how it works *before* you tackle the one on the speedometer you want to fit to your car.

**If you want to set the odometer on a replacement movement to agree with your car's actual mileage you have to take it apart. 'Winding' the movement back or forwards will only break it**

Above **The dials on an odometer are driven by either 10:1 epicyclic gears (as shown) or by small pins and pips on the edges of the dial drums**

Below **On this type of trip odometer the setting adjustment moves a spring-loaded centre spindle sideways to take the drive gear out of engagement. If the trip does not work, this spring may be weak or corroded**

Below right **An alternative type of trip odometer uses a ratchet drive, and the zeroing adjuster moves the pawl out of engagement**

Where there are two mileage-recording drums, one for the total mileage of the car and the other for 'trip' mileages, the drive to the trip recorder is arranged so that you can, by either pushing or pulling on the resetting shaft, disengage the drive and rotate it back to zero. Once again, there are different methods of arranging the drive between the two sets of drums, but it is always quite a simple mechanism and not difficult to understand when you study it.

## Rev counters

Mechanically-driven tachometers, or rev counters, are often driven from a cable on the back of the dynamo or distributor shaft, and the same points apply here as to

Top **Some trip zeroing controls screw on to the end of the adjustment shaft**

Above **With another type of trip zeroing control there is a small hole and a split pin to engage the control with the shaft**

speedometer drives. A possible, though not very likely, cause of an inaccurate reading with a mechanically-driven tachometer is the use of a wrong-size fan pulley or a wrong-ratio gearbox behind the drive from the engine. If the needle of a mechanically-driven tachometer seems reasonably accurate at low revs but lags behind at high revs on a dynamo-driven cable, the trouble is most likely to be due to a slipping fan belt.

During the 1940s, electric tachometers were also developed, and in the 1950s and 1960s were used on cars such as Jaguars, Lagondas and the like. They did not need a cable to drive them, but they had to have an electric generator driven by the engine, often from the back of the camshaft, and were not really suitable as add-on

instruments because of the difficulties of arranging the drive.

If you perceive no reading at all on this type of instrument, you can check whether the fault lies with the instrument, the generator or in the wiring, by using an AC voltmeter. It must be an AC voltmeter, or a multimeter set to read AC volts, as a DC-reading voltmeter will be completely misleading. Take the wiring off the generator and check the voltage across its terminals with the engine

On yet another type, the trip zeroing control screws into a boss alongside the main drive boss

running. It should be something in the order of one volt for every 100 engine rpm. If all is well here, reconnect the cables to the generator, disconnect them from the instrument and check the voltage reading at the instrument end of the cables. No voltage here means that the trouble is somewhere in the cables. If there is a voltage reading here but you still get nothing from the instrument then the instrument itself is faulty. The instruments are basically moving-coil AC voltmeters, and other than ensuring that the terminals are clean, there is little you can do to repair them satisfactorily at home.

Should you decide to look for one in a breaker's yard or autojumble rather than send your own away for repair, be careful to get one that is calibrated to suit your generator. It does not follow, even though they may look similar, that tachometer generators from different makes of car all deliver the same voltage for the same rotational speed. To be on the safe side, get one that was originally used with your engine or the calibration may be very inaccurate.

Later electronic impulse tachometers (and these include proprietary add-on units) work on a totally different principle from the electric ones. There are two types of electronic instrument, those which sense the current pulses in the ignition system and those which sense the voltage changes. Most impulse tachometers need a special adaptor to allow them to work with electronic ignition systems, so if you are planning to fit one as an add-on instrument, or if you are fitting an electronic ignition system, check with the maker of the tachometer whether or not you will need an adaptor. The cheaper electronic tachometers are designed to work only on four-, six- or eight-cylinder engines, so if you are looking for a replacement head, make sure you get one with the right count. Most, though by no means all, of the more expensive ones are adjustable at the back of the instrument. If you are looking for a replacement, check also that the one you get is suitable for positive *and* negative earth systems. Or if it is for one system only, make sure that you get the right one appropriate to your car.

Wiring for these instruments is quite simple and will be given either in the car's wiring diagram or in a leaflet with

the proprietary instrument. Both types need a power supply which is taken from the terminal for auxiliaries which is controlled by the ignition switch. There is a point to bear in mind, which may easily lead to confusion, should the tachometer not seem to be working. It might be designed to be powered by the full 12 volts of your car's supply, or it might possibly be designed to take its operating power from the output side of the voltage stabilizer which feeds the other instruments. In this case it might be designed to operate from a power supply of 9 or 10 volts, and you could damage it if you run it with the full 12 volts across it for very long. The tachometer will, of

**Unless you are well versed in electronics there is little you can do at home if one of the components inside an electronic tachometer fails**

course, fail together with the other instruments, should the voltage stabilizer fail.

Separate from the power supply to the instrument is the sensing. On current-sensing types the low-tension feed from the ignition coil to the side of the distributor is interrupted and fed through a sensing loop inside the instrument, so you have two sensing terminals at the back, one 'in' and one 'out'. The type which senses voltage changes has only one sensing lead from the back of the instrument. This goes to the low-tension terminal on the ignition coil which feeds the distributor. If your car is fitted with a ballasted ignition system the coil will be designed to run normally at about 9 volts, fed through the ballast resistor. When you operate the starter, the ballast resistor is bypassed by a lead from the starter solenoid and the coil overruns at full battery voltage to give a good spark for starting. Many voltage-sensing impulse tachometers are quite happy taking their impulse at anything from 8 to 14 volts, but if you are looking for a replacement head, do check before you fit it.

As with electric tachometers, home repairs on electronic impulse-counting types are seldom successful. There is, however, one possible fault that you can check on these instruments. Sometimes the feed cable in the back of the instrument is pulled so tightly that it distorts a plastic former inside. The cable must pass through an iron core inside the instrument in a nice easy curve.

# Chapter 4 | Electric fuel and temperature gauges

Though repair of speedometers and tachometers is best handled by a specialist firm, there is a lot you can do at home to repair and restore the auxiliary instruments, or even transfer the guts of a second-hand working one into your casing if you cannot find a second-hand instrument which exactly matches your dial display.

We will look first at fuel gauges and electrically-operated coolant temperature gauges, as these illustrate the two basic types of electrically-operated instrument, the

**Failure of several auxiliary instruments may be because the voltage stabilizer has failed. This is the component at the top left of this instrument cluster, but not all stabilizers are so easy to reach**

moving-iron type where you get a reading the instant you switch on, and the bimetallic-strip type which takes a few seconds to 'warm up' and reach its reading, but has the advantage that the needle does not bounce about. The moving-iron type may be connected through a voltage stabilizer, but this is not usual. The bimetallic-strip instruments usually are connected through a stabilizer.

This voltage stabilizer keeps a constant voltage at the instrument, usually 10 volts, so that the reading is not affected by fluctuating battery voltage. By checking on the wiring diagram for your car, in the handbook or manual, you will see whether or not you have a stabilizer. If you have, it often serves more than one instrument, so if several go dead at the same time, the stabilizer is the prime suspect.

Unfortunately, many stabilizers are tucked away in inconvenient positions behind the fascia but once you get at them they can easily be checked with a voltmeter. First, check the voltage on the input side to make sure that it is connected to the car's electrical supply, then check the voltage at the output terminal, the one which goes to the instruments. Disconnect the output cable for these checks so you will not be misled either by a faulty instrument or by a fault in the cable. If the stabilizer checks out all right, your second check should be for any short-circuits in the wiring, from the stabilizer to the instruments. Check also, from your car's wiring diagram, whether or not the cases of the instruments have to be connected to chassis earth. Sometimes it is not necessary, but if this is so and the earthing strap from them is broken, then you will get either no reading at all or a very misleading reading. Do these checks even if the stabilizer has burned out, because a short-circuit either in the instrument itself or in the wiring from the stabilizer to the instrument could be the reason for the stabilizer burning, and if so a new one will not last very long.

The moving-iron type of instrument jumps up to a reading and back again to 'Empty' or 'Cold' as soon as you switch on and off. It is not used very often for temperature gauges, but was the standard type of fuel gauge a few years ago. There are two terminals at the back of it, one fed from the ignition switch and one going to the tank unit or the

On instruments with die-cast cases, you may have to clean corrosion round the edge before the movement will lift out

temperature-sending unit. The casing may be connected to earth, so once again, check with your car's wiring diagram.

If the instrument does not work, and all the connections seem good, check the voltage at the input terminal, often marked B for Battery. The second terminal is often marked T for Tank or Temperature and is connected via these units to earth. If, when you switch on, the needle jumps over to 'Full' or 'Hot', it is a pretty sure sign that this lead is shorting out to earth somewhere, or that the tank unit or temperature sensor itself is shorting out to earth. Check by disconnecting the cable from it and if the cable is not shorting the reading should drop back to zero. On the other hand, if the reading stays at 'Full' or 'Hot' then the cable is probably shorting somewhere along its run. However, should you get not even a flicker when you switch on and you are getting voltage to the B terminal on the instrument, then disconnect the cable from the T terminal and use a short jumper lead from this terminal to earth. If the needle now gives a full reading the chances are that the instrument is all right, and your trouble is either the tank unit or sender, or a break in the cable to either of these units.

To find out which, reconnect the cable at the T terminal and take the other end off the tank unit or sender. If you now earth this end you should get a 'Full' reading, in which case the fault is in the unit. If you do not, the fault is in the cable. For safety's sake, it is advisable to disconnect the battery while you make and remake connections around the petrol tank. It is a lot of trouble to do this every time

The movement of a cheap bimetallic instrument. Most troubles are due to corrosion and bad contact where the fine wires are soldered to their terminals

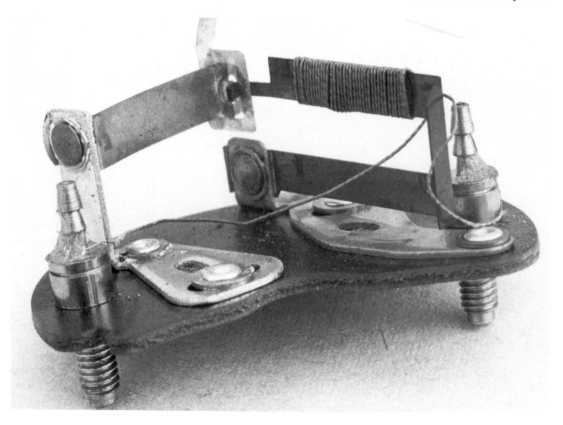

you make or remake a connection, but the unit is often near the tank breather pipe, and it takes only a very small spark to set off petrol vapour and cause an explosion.

Before you finally decide that the tank unit or temperature sender is at fault, check that the body of it is earthing properly. With a temperature-sending unit which has been weeping slightly and has dried crystals of antifreeze around it, it is possible that these crystals have insulated or partly insulated the thread in the body of the sender unit from the engine or thermostat housing into which it is screwed. With a tank unit, the earth is made through the fixing screws and though it is unlikely that all of them are making bad contact with the tank, sometimes you may find that the fault is that the tank itself is not making good contact with the chassis. This may be because its mountings are corroded or it may be that it is mounted through rubber bushes and the earthing strap from the tank to the car's chassis or body has broken.

If you still get no results after making all these checks, the fault *must* be with the unit itself. There is little or nothing you can do with a faulty temperature sender except to make certain it *is* faulty, by running a slave lead from its terminal to the T terminal on the gauge and by immersing the sender in hot water. It does not matter about getting it wet, but remember that you must have another lead from the body of the sender to chassis earth on the car.

If you are thinking about hunting for a second-hand sender at an autojumble or breaker's yard, remember that there are three types which correspond to three types of instruments: the moving-iron type and two bimetallic-strip types. On the first bimetallic type, which with Smiths Instruments is coded TE somewhere on the dial, the pointer rises slowly to 'Hot' when you switch off. This type is seldom used with a voltage stabilizer. On the second type, which Smiths code BT, the pointer drops slowly to 'Cold' when you switch off. This type must be used with a voltage stabilizer as the full 12 volts across its terminals will soon burn it out. It is important to use the correct matching type of sender unit.

As a guide—and it must be regarded *only* as a guide—the Smiths sender for the first type of bimetallic gauge usually has a parallel thread and a lock nut on the body. The sender for the second type usually has a taper thread and no lock nut. I know of no special identifying features on the senders for moving-iron gauges. In each case, if you are hunting for a second-hand one it is wise, if you can, to check against the instrument to which it was originally sending its messages.

Fuel tank units, on the other hand, often respond to a little love and kindness, and restoration. Take the unit out of the tank, and take it well away from the tank before you start making any connections just in case you produce a spark. It is also a good idea to cover the hole in the tank, both for safety reasons and to stop dirt getting in. Take the unit up front where you can see the gauge and bypass all the other wiring by taking one cable from the tank terminal to the T terminal on the gauge and another from the body of the tank unit to chassis earth. Switch on, and watch for any indications on the gauge when you move the float arm to

**Repairs to a leaking metal tank unit float can be made with soft solder**

send the slider across the resistance. The instrument is basically an ammeter, and responds to changes in current depending on the value of the resistance offered by the tank unit between the cable and earth.

There are four faults to look for. The float could have been punctured and not floating, the resistance wire and the slider contact could be dirty, the resistance could be disconnected either from the terminal or, at its other end, from the body of the unit, or the terminal could be shorting out to earth because its insulation washer has perished.

If the float is punctured there will be petrol slopping about inside it, and with a metal float you have to get rid of this completely before you can solder it. You cannot repair a punctured plastic float. Find the puncture by immersing the float in hot water—but take the hot water well away from any flame because of the possible presence of petrol vapour. The puncture will show up as a stream of tiny bubbles, just like the bubbles from a punctured inner tube,

**Most troubles with fuel tank units are either due to corrosion on the resistance coil, or that one of the ends of the resistance wire has broken at its terminal**

except that these will be petrol vapour and not just air. Mark the puncture, and keep on immersing the float in hot water until no more bubbles come out. If necessary, enlarge the puncture slightly with a point to make things easier for a repair. When no more bubbles come out, dry the float, let it cool down and clean the area of the puncture with emery-cloth. Then repair the puncture with a smear of solder. Use an electric soldering iron, not a flame, as many of these metal floats are constructed with soft solder, and if you use a flame you are likely to see it fall to pieces in front of your eyes. Use a resin-cored solder, the sort sold for electrical work, rather than plain solder and killed spirit flux. The float will be slightly heavier because of the solder, but this will not affect the reading to any great extent.

Coping with a broken connection at either end of the resistance, or a short between the terminal and the body, is

**On this ammeter the movement lifts away from the outer casing after unclamping a thin metal strap**

On a moving-iron ammeter the control coil is of heavy gauge wire. It is built to take currents up to 30 amps or more, but even so, a dead short of the main electric feed could burn it out

pretty straightforward, which leaves only a dirty resistance and slider contact to be investigated. Sometimes, if the unit has been standing for a few years, these get too dirty to make good contact and sometimes they are dirty at the 'Full' end of the resistance because it is years since anyone filled the tank more than half-full. Clean the resistance wire with the finest wet-and-dry rubbing paper, brush the dust away and then, after spraying it with switch cleaner, work the slider back and forth a few times. These switch cleaners are usually trichloroethane or carbon tetrachloride. These are non-flammable so you do not have to worry about electric sparks afterwards, but avoid breathing the vapour which can be harmful to your lungs. *Never smoke* while you are using these as the vapour can turn into a very nasty poisonous gas when drawn through the hot end of a cigarette or pipe. I will deal with repairs to the instruments themselves in a later chapter.

Ammeters are almost all the moving-iron type, but as they have to carry anything up to 35 or 40 amps, the coil

Right **On this type of ammeter the pointer is controlled by a soft iron disc running in a ring coil**

Below **This fuel gauge was not working because one of the terminals was shorting out against the casing**

inside is wound from quite thick gauge wire and burns out only if it has been severely mistreated. The most likely cause of a moving-iron ammeter burning out is if someone has connected it directly across a battery to see if it works. In a dead-short condition such as this, the battery will deliver anything up to 300 amps or more and the ammeter probably would work for a second or two before the coil burnt out, so never test an ammeter in this way.

The iron sector piece under the pointer is usually arranged to move inside the coil instead of in the magnetic field of the two pole pieces as with moving-iron temperature and fuel gauges. In a few high-quality older cars you might find a high-grade moving-coil ammeter. These work on the principle of a coil of wire inside an iron sector, moving in the magnetic field created by the current. They are more accurate than the moving-iron type, but are more delicate and more prone to failure from shocks and jars. Should they become deranged inside, it is difficult to repair them at home, and difficult to calibrate them without rigging up a test bench with another, accurate ammeter for comparison.

A typical fuel-gauge movement, with the pointer controlled by a pair of coils

Battery-condition indicators are voltmeters connected, usually via the control box or possibly the starter solenoid, across the terminals of the battery. Basically these are ammeters with a resistance built into them, so that the current is cut down to a figure where the instrument can handle it. A few older ones were made in the same way as moving-iron ammeters, but many of the later ones are simple bimetallic-strip instruments very similar inside to temperature and fuel gauges except for the resistance.

# Chapter 5 | Bourdon tube gauges

The Bourdon tube principle is used in mechanically-operated oil-pressure gauges, vacuum gauges and the type of temperature gauge which has a long capillary tube running from the instrument to a sensing bulb at the other end, which is usually fitted either to the radiator header tank or to part of the engine block. The Bourdon tube oil-pressure gauge is connected by a pipe to a take-off point on the main oil gallery of the engine, and in the case of a vacuum gauge the connection is to a take-off point on the inlet manifold, usually just below the carburettor.

The principle of a Bourdon tube gauge is very simple and is basically the same as the type of party novelty

**There are a number of ways in which Bourdon tube movements are held in their cases. This one uses three screws through the case side**

Another method of holding a
Bourdon tube movement is by a
nut on the connecting thread

Instead of a nut you may find a
screwed collar which needs a
fork spanner with two turned-
down prongs to undo it

squeaker which you blow at one end, and which unrolls
under the pressure of your blow. Inside the Bourdon tube
instrument is a flattened tube bent in an arc, sealed at one
end and with the other end connected to the pressure pipe.
As the pressure in the pipe increases, the curved tube tries

There are two types of ends to the connectors of Bourdon tube gauges. This one takes a flat nipple with a leather washer

The other type of Bourdon connector uses an olive on the pipe with no washer

to straighten out or, in the case of a vacuum gauge, as the pressure in the pipe falls the tube tends to curl into a tighter arc. This movement of the tube moves the pointer on the dial. In the case of the oil-pressure gauge, the pressure is generated by the pressure in the engine's main oil gallery. However, with a vacuum gauge the drop in pressure is the depression in the inlet manifold, while in a temperature

Inside the case of a Bourdon
tube oil-pressure gauge there is
often an adjustable guard stop
to restrain the tube when the oil
is cold and thick and at very
high pressure

gauge pressure is generated by ether in a sensor bulb
heating up and expanding as a vapour.

There are two qualities of Bourdon tube instruments.
The older, better-quality type has the Bourdon tube
connected to the pointer by a small delicate linkage with a
toothed rack. The spindle for the pointer has a pinion on it
and it is damped by a balance spring like a watch balance
spring. On the later, cheaper type, the Bourdon tube is
connected to the pointer by a rather crude lever linkage,

Right **A good-quality Bourdon tube movement with a rack-and-pinion action**

Below **The much cheaper type of Bourdon tube movement has just a bent wire link**

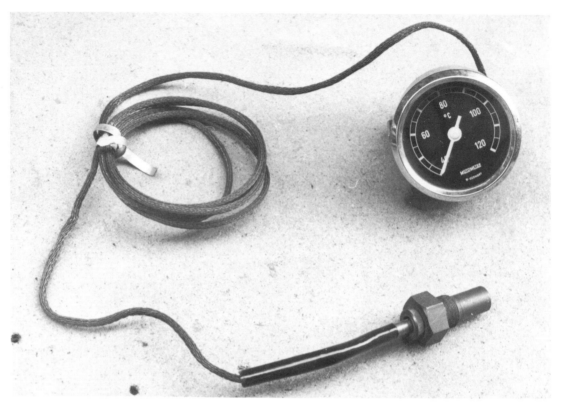

The type of temperature gauge
which has a capillary tube
linking it to the sensor. If this
tube breaks, the system will have
to be refilled with ether

and pointer damping is looked after by a long coiled spring wound loosely round the pointer spindle. The better-quality instrument is the more accurate and responds more readily to small variations in pressure, but on a car we are not looking for laboratory degrees of accuracy, and the cheaper type is robust and records sufficiently accurately for our purposes.

If the Bourdon tube develops a leak, as it occasionally does, it can usually be soldered quite readily, and the solder is flexible enough not to affect the reading to any extent, but in the case of a temperature gauge the ether which generates the pressure will have been lost, so the unit has to be refilled. It will also have to be refilled if the capillary tube breaks. Normally, these capillary tubes are generously long and when they break they usually do so at one of the ends, so there is almost always enough length left over to remake the connection.

Resoldering the tube either to the sensor bulb or to the block at the end of the Bourdon tube in the instrument is a reasonably straightforward job provided you do not block the capillary tube with solder. It has a very fine bore and easily becomes blocked. Also at the instrument end there is a second short length of tube soldered into the block. This is the filling tube and its free end will be sealed with a blob of solder. To refill the instrument you have to unsolder this end or nip it off if it is long enough, or if the tube is too short you should replace it with a longer piece cut either from a scrap capillary tube or from the capillary tube of the instrument, provided you have enough to spare.

To fill the instrument you will need about two to three fluid ounces of ether, preferably a little more to allow for losses by evaporation. Commercial-quality ether is quite suitable, but you will probably have to get the medical quality from a chemist. The chemist may wonder why you want it and will probably ask you, but if you explain why you need it you ought not to have a lot of trouble getting it.

Handling ether is perfectly safe provided you take sensible precautions. The first precaution is obviously not to work in a confined space where the fumes can affect you. It is, after all, quite a powerful anaesthetic. The second safety precaution is that ether constitutes a serious fire hazard if there are any naked flames about, and it is only too easy to forget such things as pilot lights on gas cookers or gas refrigerators. Electric fires of the type on which the element glows red can also present a fire hazard if you are working with an inflammable liquid as volatile as ether. Work in a well-ventilated area and use an electric kettle or electric hot plate for heating.

When you are ready, heat the sensor bulb in boiling water and hold the end of the filling tube under the ether. Bubbles will start coming out as the air in the bulb expands. When they stop, transfer the sensor bulb to cold water without lifting the filling tube from the ether. As the bulb cools it will draw ether in. Repeat this process and continue it until the bulb is full of ether—or as full as you can get it. The flow of bubbles will never stop entirely, but it will get slightly less as the volume of air inside gets smaller, until you come to the point where only a few

The sensor is often in two parts, a housing which screws into the radiator or thermostat which also contains the inner sensing bulb

bubbles appear which will be vaporized ether. Now, while still keeping the filling tube immersed in ether, immerse the bulb in water at freezing temperature (you can achieve this by using crushed ice from the refrigerator) to lessen the chance of the ether expanding and flowing out, crimp the end of the tube with a pair of pliers, then lift it out of the ether and solder the end to seal it.

Finally, you will have to recalibrate. You must do this at boiling point because the pointer will return back to its stop well before the temperature of the bulb gets anywhere near to freezing point. Put the sensor bulb in boiling water and leave it there for a couple of minutes to stabilize the reading. If the pointer comes up to the 'Hot' mark on the dial, or well into the red sector if the dial has only coloured indications, all is probably well, but the chances are that you will not have got exactly the same amount of ether in the bulb as it originally had, so if the indication is badly wrong you have to take the pointer off and reset it while the bulb is still in the boiling water. You may not have the most scientifically accurate temperature-recording instrument in the world, but at least it will work and it will be as accurate as most of the cheaper, modern electric types. When you refit it to the car, coil any excess capillary tube into loops, hold them together with a piece of tape and suspend them vertically. They absorb vibration better vertically than when they are laid horizontally.

With oil-pressure gauges and vacuum gauges, there is a point to watch if you are looking for a second-hand one or using the insides of one that you have picked up at an

autojumble to fit into your own casing, to match the other instruments. These pressure gauges and vacuum gauges have two types of connector at the back. One is countersunk and takes a cone-shaped nipple on the end of the pressure pipe; the other is flat with a small raised pip in the middle and it takes a flat-ended nipple with a fibre washer. The wrong type of nipple used on either type of gauge will leak.

In this case the inner sensing bulb also holds the small filling tube

# Chapter 6 | Repairing instruments, switches and cables

The sort of instruments which are grouped round a single dial usually unbolt quite easily, and in the case of separate circular instruments the bezel at the front usually comes off after a quarter turn is made. On some types of grouped instruments—the auxiliary instruments on Ford Anglias and Prefects from the 1950s are a good case in point—you will find that when you take the instrument out of the main group cluster the dial is riveted on to a cover plate. Do not attempt to take the dial off this plate as it is very thin, and you will undoubtedly buckle it in the attempt. The cover plate itself can be taken off by turning up the small rivet tags at the two holes where the instrument bolts through to the main housing. Sometimes the dial may be removed without disturbing the pointer.

On some grouped auxiliary instruments the dial is carried on two plastic pillars, to which it is riveted. Once again, do not attempt to lever the dial off, or you will buckle it. In most cases the plastic pillars are a tight, push fit on two pins in the body of the instrument and if you lever carefully with a small screwdriver you should be able to lift the dial and the pillars away without disturbing the small dial rivets. Lever each pillar up a little at a time or you will crease the dial. In some cases you will have to take the pointer off if you want to remove the dial.

Take care how you do this. The pointer will pull straight upwards off its spindle, but it may be tight and if you bend the spindle or break the spindle bearings you will never be able to repair either.

There are two types of pointers: the type with a blind hole which fits over the end of the spindle, and the type where the hole goes right through, so that the spindle pokes

Above **On a large instrument cluster there may be felt pads to stop warning lights from reflecting all over the cluster. They often drop out when you take off the cover**

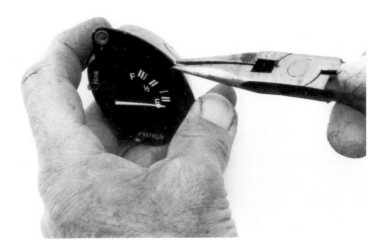

Right **In a few cases there are clips, as well as rivets, holding the dial of an auxiliary instrument to the case**

Right **If the hollow dial rivets are bifurcated and crimped over, they can be levered up with a small screwdriver**

Below right **With non-bifurcated dial rivets you will have to file one side off**

**If the dial is riveted to plastic pillars it is easier to lever the pillar off its stud, than to extract the rivet**

**After filing or uncrimping you can push the rivet out with the tang of a file**

out the top of the centre boss. To take off the second type of pointer, instrument repairers use a small tool which is in effect a two-arm claw puller. You can buy these from companies which supply tools to the watch- and clock-repairing trade. For the other type of pointer, repairers usually use two small levers which, again, you can buy, or you can quite easily make up yourself. You can, of course, use the two levers to take off the second type of pointer as well, but unless you have the fulcrum jig used by instrument repairers, you will have to rely on the sides of

Right **Professional repairers use a miniature claw puller to take pointers off**

Below **A pointer can be taken off with two levers, but watch that it does not fly up suddenly and get lost**

The two smaller nuts on the back of this fuel gauge hold the coils, and the slots in the casing are for adjusting their position. If you have to move them mark their position, otherwise, without measuring instruments, you will have to adjust by trial and error

the instrument case to provide purchase for the levers. Some pointers are quite tight, particularly if the instrument is a few years old, so be prepared for it to fly up into the air when it comes free. It is useful to ask a helper to hold a hand loosely over the top while you lever the pointer off otherwise you may spend quite a long time hunting for it on the floor.

Sometimes the dial will lift straight out of the instrument case complete with the plastic ring over the lighting windows, but in other cases you may have to either take out two tiny screws or unbend some crimped-over tags. On a few instruments (earlier Morris Minors for example), the instrument cases are cast in Mazak, so be prepared for the tags to break off. If they do this, the dial can later be held in place with just a *spot* of non-setting adhesive such as rubber solution. It will not work loose once the case is done up again, but it will be quite easy to take off should you want to go inside again at some future date.

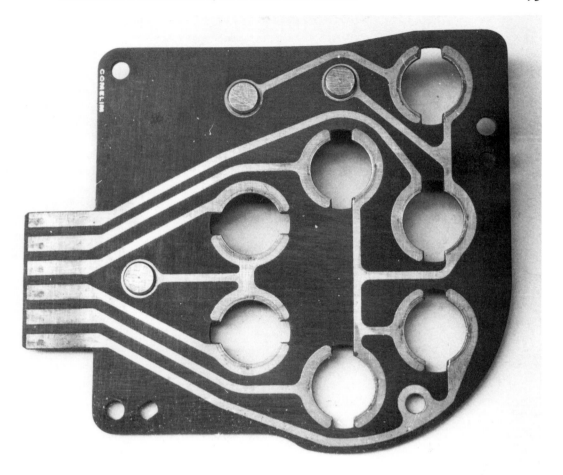

On moving-iron-type fuel gauges and temperature gauges try not to disturb the two nuts which hold the bias coils to the back of the case. These are usually just below the terminal nuts and there are slots in the case to adjust the coil positions. These coils are joined with fine hair-like wires, and apart from the difficulty of lining them up again properly, it is very easy to break the connection between them.

If the coils have been disturbed by someone else and the fine wire is broken, you can have a go at soldering it back again, but you need a very fine soldering iron indeed. Even the fine sort sold for radio and electronics work is usually

In the last ten years or so, printed circuits have been used in place of instrument wiring. If you find a break in the circuit it can be repaired by soldering a wire bridge across

too thick, so wrap a piece of copper wire about $\frac{1}{16}$ in. diameter round the solder bit, and lead it off the bottom to make an auxiliary soldering bit. If you file a slight screwdriver end to it you will find you have a very fine bit. After soldering, you may have to reset the coil positions. Without a test bench, the only way to do this is by guess and trial and error, moving each one a fraction at a time while the instrument is connected. In the case of a fuel gauge you can move the float arc up and down to get the pointer to move, and in the case of a temperature gauge you can put the sensor bulb alternately in hot and cold water. The coils will probably not finish up exactly symmetrical, and the instrument may not be as accurate as when it left the factory, but at least it will give you a pretty good indication—which is what most temperature and fuel gauges give, anyway.

In a few moving-coil instruments (more modern Jaguars for example), the layout of the coils is different. In this case you have one coil overlapping the other and both the coils and the pointer are carried on a self-contained sub-assembly. The whole lot is crimped together, and if anything is burnt out the only thing to do is replace the instrument or the complete sub-assembly from another similar instrument.

Modern bimetallic instruments are very cheaply mass-produced and the insides, though they may be a triumph for the production engineer, are very difficult to repair should anything burn out. About the only thing you can do, apart from replacing the complete insides, is to solder back the end of the fine wire which wraps round the bimetallic strip should it have come adrift.

If you are looking for a second-hand instrument to replace one of yours, or for an instrument from which you can take the insides to put in your casing, there are several things to bear in mind. The first is to find out whether or not the replacement instrument originally worked through a voltage stabilizer. If it did, and your car does not have a voltage stabilizer, the instrument may stand up to the 12 volts instead of the 10 for which it was stabilized—but in the case of bimetallic-strip instruments, the operation of the instrument depends on variations in current, and the

**Above** If the bit on your soldering iron is too large and clumsy you can extend it with thinner copper wire wound tightly round it

**Top** You need a very fine iron to do any soldering repairs inside an instrument

voltage stabilizer is there to keep the voltage constant. If both the current and the voltage vary, as they will do without a voltage stabilizer, the instrument will give quite inaccurate readings depending on the state of charge of your battery. It is also important in the case of bimetallic temperature gauges to check the code number, either TE or BT with Smiths Instruments. The actual code number may not be the same, as the instrument may well be coded according to the type of dial fitted to it or even according to which car it was intended to fit. But the capital letters ought to be the same.

This dial suffered from having a broken glass while the car was standing idle for three years. It needs rewriting or replacing

MADE IN ENGLAND

The second thing to look for is the full-scale deflection of the pointer, often referred to as its FSD. Some instruments, particularly some oil-pressure gauges, have an FSD of about 270 degrees, while others may have an FSD of about 60 degrees. If you are replacing one instrument of a grouped set in a large dial the same size as the speedometer, getting the FSD right is important. If, however, you are replacing a separate instrument, you need not worry too much about the FSD, though if it is different from the one on your original instrument you will have to make a new dial or the readings will be inaccurate. The separate instruments with the smaller FSD quite often had the same insides as the ones fitted to the grouped-dial type in the interests of quantity production, and it is quite likely that you will be able to take the insides from one instrument and swap them over to the other without too much difficulty. Once again, though, you will have to make a new dial if your original is damaged.

A professional dial restorer will be able to reletter a dial by hand so that you are unable to tell the difference between his work and the original, but this is highly skilled, expensive work requiring long practice to achieve. However, there are various other ways of doing the job at home which require less skill and which result in a job which requires very close inspection indeed to be able to distinguish from the original.

In the case of black-on-white, or white-on-black, dials which are front-lit through small windows at the side of the instrument case, the easiest way to reproduce a dial is photographically. You will need a camera with either a macro lens or extension tubes for close focusing, and if you do not possess this equipment yourself there are many amateur photographers who do and who will be only too pleased to try their skills on a spot of copying. Try your local photographic society. It is best if you can use a copying stand to make sure that the camera is completely square with the dial you are copying, but with care you can manage without it. This presupposes that you have access to a dial which can be copied. If you are a member of a one-make club, or you have a friend with a car of a similar model to yours or with identical instruments, you will probably not have a great deal of difficulty persuading them to allow you to borrow an instrument to photograph it. You will need to take off the bezel and glass, but it is not advisable to take the pointer off a borrowed instrument as it is quite easy to damage it, and if it is damped by a hairspring you may have difficulty getting it back to the correct calibration. The pointer will show on your finished print but in most cases, particularly with white-on-black instruments, it is not difficult to touch this out provided you arrange things so that the pointer does not cover the instrument maker's trademark. When the finished print is being made you can lay your original dial on the enlarger baseboard to make sure that the reproduction dial is exactly the same size. Generally, a matt-surfaced printing paper produces a better-looking dial than either the glossy or stippled 'pearl'-surfaced papers. The finished dial can then be cut out and stuck on top of your original, with an adhesive such as Cow Gum.

Photographing a similar instrument is a good way of reproducing a black dial with white lettering. The pointer can be touched out after printing

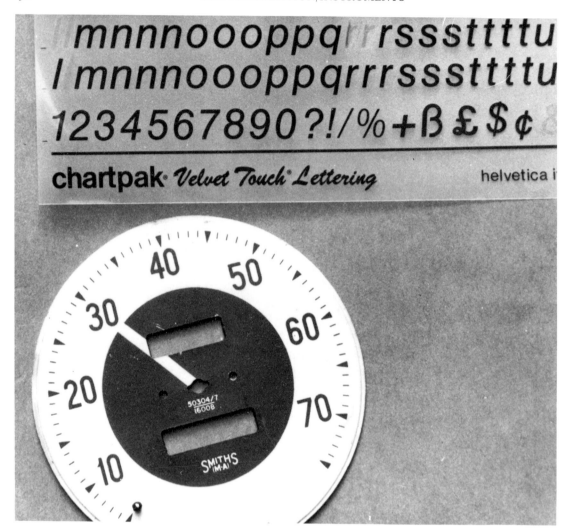

**Try your local stationers or art shop for rub-down lettering to rewrite a dial. In this case the dial is lettered with Helvetica Medium, but the lettering on the transfer sheet is Helvetica Medium italic**

Instruments which have a translucent plastic dial which is lit from behind present a little more difficulty. It is possible, though not very easy, to obtain sheets of sensitized photographic film with a frosted translucent finish which is used in the same way as photographic printing paper. The dial can be photographed and reproduced on this, but there are two possible snags. The first is that this sensitized film is much thinner than the original plastic dial and you may have difficulty in fitting it to lie flat in the instrument case. The second difficulty is that many of these back-lit instruments had the figures and scale reproduced in brown, while the normal reproduction on sensitized film will be black. It may be possible to tone the finished film print to a brown colour to match the original dial, but this is something on which you would have to consult the film maker. You will find the technical departments of film makers such as Kodak and Agfa very helpful, if you explain what you are trying to do.

The alternative is to reletter the original dial with a rub-down transfer lettering such as Letraset. Rub-down transfer lettering is produced in a wide variety of type-faces and you should be able to find one which matches your instrument, as near as makes very little difference. Once again you may be faced with the colour difficulty as most rub-down lettering is black not brown, but there are firms making coloured rub-down lettering which is used in colour display work. Though you may not be able to obtain it from your local stationers, it may well be listed in the catalogue and they can order it for you. One point to remember is that the rub-down lettering will not stick properly to the face of a plastic dial unless you get rid of any trace of grease on the dial, and this includes ordinary fingermarks. Be careful which solvent and cleaner you use to get rid of any grease spots on the dial as some solvents are likely to take off the rest of the lettering, and if possible it is better to use rub-down transfer lettering over the top of the original damaged lettering to get the figures in exactly the same place. Probably the best thing to clean a dial of this sort with is lukewarm water with just a spot of washing-up liquid to shift the grease.

Replacing the strip of plastic on front-lit instrument windows ought not to present much difficulty as you can buy the strip, either clear or tinted to suit your original, from most model shops and some arts and handicraft shops, and as most instruments are made to one of several standard sizes, you ought not to have much trouble finding a replacement glass if necessary, either domed or flat, nor a replacement bezel.

The best way to deal with switches which are not making good contact is to find an identical replacement, but if this

**If the lighting window needs replacing it can be cut from plastic sheet bought from a model shop**

proves difficult it is sometimes possible to make a good job of repairing the original, depending on what has gone wrong inside it.

In some cases, if contact is a little uncertain but the switch sometimes works and sometimes doesn't, a squirt of switch cleaner to the insides may well do the trick. You can buy switch cleaner in aerosol cans from many radio and hi-fi shops, and it usually comes complete with a fine plastic tube which fits into the aerosol button so that you can direct the cleaner through the small gaps which you will usually find in the cover of the switch. If this does not do the trick, then the switch will have to come apart for repair.

Push-pull switches are usually the easiest to repair. The principle is very simple. There are two, or sometimes more, sets of spring contacts inside and there are a series of connecting washers on the centre push-pull piece which are insulated from the main body of the spindle. Their only

Left **Where heavy crimping makes a switch difficult to get apart without damage, squirting with switch cleaner often provides a solution to uncertain contact**

Below **On some types of push-pull switch the knob is held on by a spring-loaded plunger**

**The component parts of a two-position 'pull and turn' switch**

purpose is to bridge the gap between the contacts when you switch on and off. There is a variation on this type of switch where the push-pull spindle has just a cone on it and when you pull it the cone pushes a pair of contacts together. Sometimes, on multi-pull switches which are usually used to control side and headlamps, the pull action is in two stages with a small rotation of the knob between the two stages. This is achieved quite simply by having a peg in the centre spindle and a key-way in which the peg runs. A not uncommon fault on this type of switch is that the peg has either come completely out, or has bent so that it does not move freely in the key-way. In either case, the trouble is usually self-evident and not too difficult to put right.

The design and internal layout of switches varies so much that it would be impossible to describe them all in detail, but they nearly all fall into three distinct groupings. These are (i) the toggle switch which may be a small switch on the dashboard or perhaps a switch mounted on the steering column, (ii) the rotary switch which is sometimes used to control the lighting and (iii) the push-pull switch which has a variant in that with some you make one pull and then turn the knob slightly to make a second pull. This type is usually used to control sidelamps and headlamps.

As a general rule, switches are not made to be taken apart and repaired, and if you can get a replacement for one

Yet another example where corrosion of the contacts caused a switch, in this case a steering column lighting switch, to become erratic. A new switch was priced at £7.95. Stripping and cleaning cost nothing but time

If cheap switches with welded plastic bodies such as these go wrong, it is not worth trying to get them apart for repair

which is not working this is by far the easiest method of dealing with things. However, some switches on older cars are difficult to match and if the switch does not work anyway, you will not do any further damage by attempting

**This type of push-pull switch often suffers from the small toggle springs becoming unhooked or broken**

to repair it. The exception is the cheap plastic-bodied type of switch where the casing has been heat-welded together. It is a waste of time trying to take these apart for repair and the only recourse should they give trouble is to throw them away and renew them.

With most other switches you can usually get to the insides after levering back some tags, or a crimped-in portion of the metal casing, which holds a plastic insulated insert. In some cases the whole body of the switch may be made of plastic and is made such that you can get it apart by springing back two tags, usually one each side. Be careful how you take switches apart because the insides are usually spring-loaded to give a positive flick action, and if you take them apart carelessly the insides will fly out and you will probably lose part of it. Once you have the switch apart you will be able to see how it works. In the case of toggle switches there is usually an arm, or a block controlled by an arm, which moves so that in the 'on' position it makes contact with a pair of studs inside. With a rotary switch you may have a circular piece of insulating material with metal studs on it, or you may have a metal disc with raised pips on it which, in the case of a multi-position switch, engage with depressions in the body to give you the different positions, as well as making the contact between the studs.

In most cases, the reason for switches not working is either that the contacts have become corroded or that the spring inside which gives the flick action has broken or sometimes just come unhooked or displaced. Depending on the type of switch, the repair needed is usually fairly obvious. When you have made the repair or cleaned the contact studs as necessary, coat the switch lightly inside with petroleum jelly which will help to stave off further corrosion of the contact studs, probably for years.

With push-pull switches the conducting part which makes contact with the studs, or sometimes with brass or copper spring leaves, is carried on a centre spindle from which it is usually insulated by a plastic collar. You may be able to take this type of switch apart by bending back some crimped-in tags or you may have to drill out some hollow

When you take rotary switches apart, be careful to keep all the springs, washers and cams in order. They can be quite a puzzle to reassemble

rivets, in which case you can replace them, when the job is finished, with small nuts and bolts. Sometimes the insulating and conducting washers are held on the centre spindle by a nut at the end, but on the cheaper type of push-pull switch the end of the spindle will be riveted over. It is better to avoid filing off this rivet as you will have to file down part of these washers in order to rivet the end of the spindle over again, and there is a danger that you will make the switch such that in the 'on' position the conducting washers do not meet the studs or leaf contacts accurately. If the contacts are corroded and you cannot get the switch completely apart to clean them, you can usually get it working again by squirting some switch cleaner inside, and then working the knob backwards and forwards. In other cases, with the leaf-spring type, you may be able to push a thin strip of emery-paper alongside the centre spindle and work the knob backwards and forwards so that the emery cleans the contact studs. If you do this, make sure that you

**As with some ignition switches, the nut at the end of push-pull switches is often locked with soft solder, which may need softening to allow removal**

The action of this headlamp dip-and-flash switch is simple, but getting in to clean it is awkward because of the crimped-over housing

wash out all the emery dust afterwards with switch cleaner or with petrol, as the abrasive on such papers is often a conducting material and it can short out the switch. Switch cleaner is safer to use than petrol for this purpose, as petrol fumes in an enclosed space such as a switch housing take a long time to evaporate, and when the switch makes contact there could possibly be a spark which will ignite the petrol fumes and literally blow the whole switch apart.

With some key-controlled switches, such as ignition switches, the inside of the switch comes apart quite easily, but with some others you may puzzle for ages how they

**Corrosion from lack of use caused this ignition switch, obtained from an autojumble, to become erratic in action**

come apart. This type, usually with the body moulded in plastic but sometimes plastic enclosed in an aluminium tube, is fastened together by a brass rivet in a blind hole. This makes the switch particularly awkward to take apart, as there is no means of extracting this pin other than to drill or file. In some cases this is relatively easy to do and in other cases it is almost impossible. If the switch is enclosed in an aluminium tubular housing, the chances of success are relatively slight, so it is best to look for another switch.

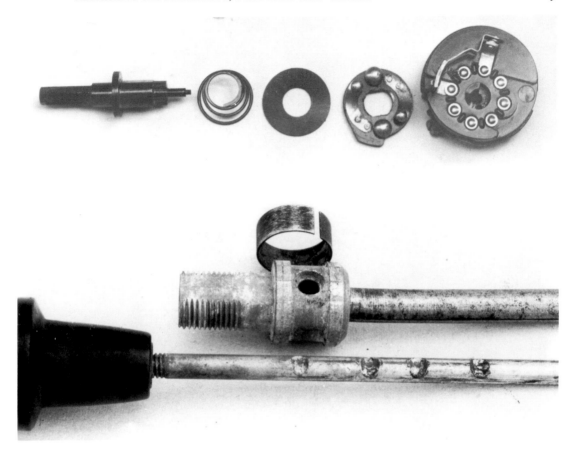

Unfortunately, if this is an ignition switch it is pointless to buy one without the key to operate it, otherwise you will have to get the blind rivet out in order to take out the lock barrel, to deal with it in the way already described in the chapter on door locks.

Choke and starter control cables often give trouble at the starter or carburettor end, where there is a tendency for the inner flexible wire to become frayed so that it is difficult to connect. In other cases the outer casing may have become kinked so that the inner cable will not move freely inside it. You may have difficulty in getting a complete control cable to match the original, but in almost all cases it is relatively easy to replace either the outer casing or the inner cable. The outer casing is usually held to the tubular part, by

Above **This choke control has notches to hold it in four positions. A plunger, spring-loaded by a spring collar, engages with the notches**

Top **The component parts of a rotary switch after cleaning. The two contact points are for the key-start solenoid**

Top **Many push-button switches can be taken apart after the end of the casing is uncrimped**

Above **A push-button starter switch taken apart. Once again corrosion had made its action erratic**

which the cable is mounted, by being crimped on—usually either with a crimped ring or with three or four crimped indentations. In some cases this tubular metal piece into which the outer casing fits is slotted, so that to remove the outer cable it is just a matter of inserting a screwdriver blade and twisting it to open the tube; but in other cases the tubing is solid so you may have to resort to drilling or filing the crimping to get the old outer casing away.

The easiest and cheapest source of supply for both outer casing and inner cable is your nearest cycle shop where you can buy either a long brake cable or sometimes the inner cable and outer casing by the metre. The easiest way of fixing a new outer casing to the tubular mounting part of the control is to sweat it in position with soft solder. Cut back the plastic or fabric outer cover of the casing for about three-eighths of an inch or so, clean up the outside of the

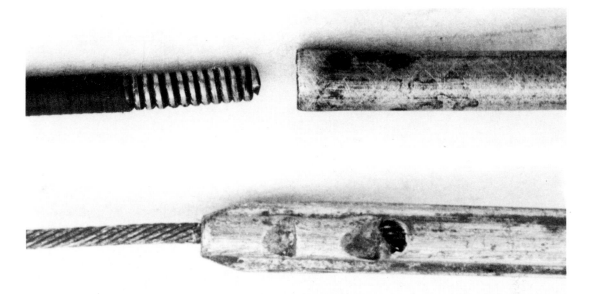

casing with emery-paper, and tin it very lightly with solder. Then clean up the inside of the tube, push the casing inside it and either lay a hot soldering iron against it or play a very small flame on it until the solder melts and the two pieces sweat together.

There are two methods of attaching the inner cable to the control part which carries the knob. The first way is by soft solder and the second is by crimping in position. If the old inner cable is sweated in, it will come out quite easily when you heat the end of the rod. If it is crimped in, then once again you may have to resort to a file to get it off. When you replace the new inner cable it is far easier to sweat it in position with soft solder, even if this is not strictly the original method.

A word on cutting stranded inner cables. If you try to cut them with nippers or side-cutters you will flatten out the end of the strands where you cut, and the chances are that you will not make a clean cut anyway, so that the cable starts to unstrand. The only way to do this job successfully is to tin it with solder for a length of about half an inch, then put it on a metal block and chop it cleanly through with a sharp, cold chisel. This will give you a clean, perfect end to

Top **To replace the outer casing of a Bowden control cable, strip the covering and soft solder it into the handle. Your local cycle shop can provide new outer casing and inner wire by the metre**

Above **The inner wire of a Bowden control is also soft-soldered through holes in the knob spindle**

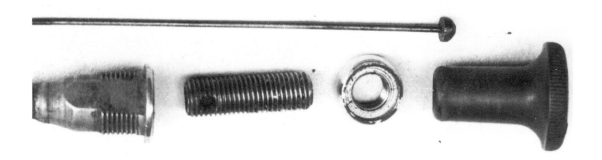

On this screw-type hand throttle control the stiff inner wire ends in a soldered-on brass mushroom which is trapped by the knob which itself screws on to the inner sleeve

the cable every time and it will not become unstranded.

In cases where the control has to work with a push and pull action, the inner cable will not be stranded—it will be a solid piece of wire. The easiest replacement for this is a length of piano wire which, even if it does not stock it, your local music shop which sells pianos will be able to get for you. Take a piece of the old wire along with you so that the shop can obtain one of the right gauge for you. Piano wire, though it is hard, will cut quite easily with a hefty pair of side-cutters. Smear the inner cable with grease before you finally push it through the outer casing, and remember that to get an easy action control cables, like speedometer drive cables, must run in easy curves and not in sharp bends.

# Chapter 7 | Window regulators

Window regulators can
sometimes seem like a Chinese
puzzle to get out of the door.
You may sometimes have to
undo bracing between the inner
and outer door skins

There are three basic types of door window regulator to be considered, but the one which you are most likely to encounter is the pinion-and-sector type, which has been fitted to millions of British cars since the early 1930s. With this type, there is a small pinion to which the handle is attached, and which drives a toothed sector. Attached to the sector is an arm ending in a metal or nylon roller which engages with a slot in the bottom of the metal piece, which

**If it has become dry and seized, the roller which engages in the glass channel develops flats and may sometimes wear right away**

is fixed to the window glass. The design of these regulators has altered very little over the years. Indeed many of the newer and older parts are interchangeable, though the fixing brackets and the length of the arm attached to the sector will vary depending on the make of car and size of door.

Getting the regulator out of the door for repair or replacement can sometimes present you with something of a puzzle. The method of fixing is simple enough, usually by four large screws to the door inner skin, and the roller on the end of the sector arm will disengage from the window when you move it to one end of its slot, where the slot is enlarged. The difficulty is encountered when you try to lift the regulator assembly out of the door through the access holes in the inner skin. In some cases this seems almost impossible to achieve, but as someone on the production line put it in, there must be a way of getting it out. In a few instances you may be able to get it out after you have undone the bottom fixing of the window channelling, or alternatively you may have to take off a stiffening bracket between the inner and outer door skins before it can be removed. Where the top part of the door is in chrome-plate or stainless steel, you may have to undo this and lift it out of the door complete with the window glass before there is room inside to wangle the regulator mechanism into a position where it can also be removed. However, do not despair if you do not succeed first time. There is always a way to get it out.

There are four main troubles which can afflict this type of regulator. The roller which engages in the bottom channelling of the window may have worn or its rivet may have come loose, the teeth on the sector may have worn, the large coil spring governing the sector and helping you to lift the window may have snapped, or the pinion which the handle turns may also have worn. These regulators are riveted together, but until recently the makers used to provide spare parts to replace those which were worn, so they were obviously assembled with a view to being taken apart for repair. Nowadays, new parts seem to be very difficult to obtain, so your best bet is to find less worn or even unworn parts from another regulator. The chances are that these will fit, even though the regulator itself will not be a direct replacement for yours. The centre spindle of

The usual type of single-arm window regulator

**Regulators for heavier windows sometimes have two arms with a pantograph action to keep the glass straight and stop it binding in its channelling**

the sector, into which the large helper spring slots, is riveted to the main mounting plate, but this riveting is usually by a cross-stake which raises four pips to hold the spindle in position. If you carefully file off these four pips, there is enough metal left to be able to re-rivet it with a punch.

The regulating arm is also riveted to the toothed sector, and if you need to fit the sector to the arm, the easiest way to get these apart is to drill out the rivets and replace them with nuts and bolts. To save these coming undone you can hammer the end of the bolt over the nut. You will probably have to grind down or file the head of the bolt to give clearance, but this should present very little difficulty if you are not intending to take out the bolt again. The housing which holds the pinion will also be riveted to the main mounting plate and once again the easiest way to get it out is to drill out the rivets. In this case you will also probably have to file or grind down the heads of at least two of the bolts you use to replace them.

Inside the housing you will find the pinion shaft, the pinion, which usually just lifts off the end of the shaft, and a large coil spring which fits into the body of the housing and

does not seem to engage with anything. It is there for two reasons. The first is to act as a flexible bush for the pinion shaft, and also to act as a damper to make it much more difficult for anyone to force down the window without turning the handle. The spring seldom gives any trouble, nor does the pinion shaft, but the teeth on the pinion sometimes wear quite badly. Fitting another pinion is just a matter of pushing it on to the end of the shaft. Pack the housing with a fairly heavy grease when you bolt it back to the regulator mounting plate, as lack of lubrication is the usual reason for the pinion and the sector wearing in the

**With some regulators you will have to drill out rivets to remove a worn pinion**

Right **A worn pinion is often the cause of window regulators slipping when the handle is turned**

Below **With other regulators the pinion housing may be held by turned-over clips**

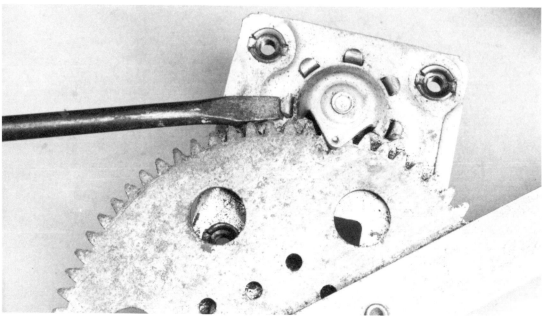

first place. Having repaired your regulator, you have to get it back into the door which can sometimes present as much of a frustrating problem as getting it out. Apart from plain manoeuvring and fiddling, there is one golden rule to remember: always engage the roller at the end of the sector arm with the slot in the glass channelling *before* you put any fixing screws back in position. If you fix the regulator in position first, or in some cases if you fix the top part of the door in position first, you will never get the roller back into its slot.

The second type of regulator you may come across is the cord-and-pulley type, though in more modern cars the cord is usually a fine stranded wire. These work on a very simple principle, though the layout of the pulley wheels may vary depending on the make of car. The way in which they work is usually quite self-evident when you inspect them, and the main faults which you will encounter are a

**The sector is also riveted to its arm, and there is often a series of holes to allow the arm to be positioned to suit different cars**

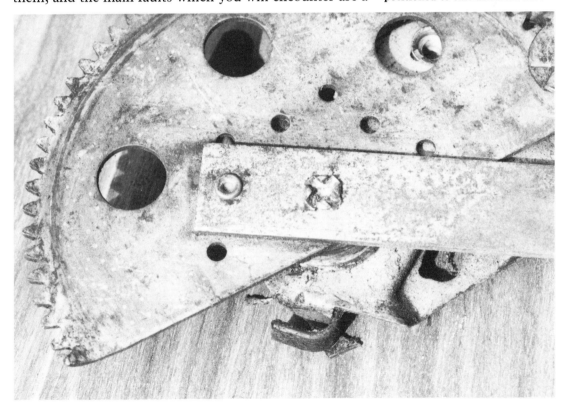

**The pinion and spindle stripped from its housing. The coil spring is merely a damper and does not hook to anything on the housing**

broken cord, a pulley which has come loose on its spindle and is wobbling badly, or a broken tension spring. On a few models this tension spring is a flat coiled spring like a clock spring, but on most it is the usual sort of sausage-shaped coil spring.

Replacing any worn or broken parts is usually quite simple, as you can always buy the flexible wire cord from any cycle shop where it is sold for making the inner cables

An older type of chain window regulator. The top chainwheel is spring-loaded to keep the chain in tension. If this spring seizes, the chain is likely to jump its cogs

of brakes and gearchange cables. As in the case of making control cables, there is only one way to cut this wire to the length you want without the ends fraying hopelessly. Mark where you want to cut it, clean it up with emery-paper and then run some solder in the strands. Then lay it on the vice or a metal stake and chop it straight through with a sharp cold chisel. Any other method of trying to cut it—with clippers, wire cutters or whatever—will leave you with the ends so frayed out and starting to unravel that you will never be able to thread it satisfactorily into position. First it is best to run an ordinary piece of cord or string round, to get the exact length you need. If the pulley spindles have worn so that the pulley wobbles and makes operation stiff and awkward, it is easiest to search for pulleys in better condition in a breaker's yard. Sometimes the spindles are bolted in position, sometimes they are riveted. If in the case of your car they are riveted, then use the old trick of drilling out the rivets, and replacing them with a nut and bolt.

The last type of window regulator is the chain type. This type is now completely obsolete, though you may still come across it if you are restoring an older car. The principle is very simple, for there is a plain chain drive, with the channelling at the bottom of the glass attached to part of the chain. One of the chain cogwheels is usually mounted in a sliding housing, and there will be either a tension or compression spring to keep tension on the chain while it is in operation, in order to prevent it jumping off the cogwheels. If the chain insists on coming off, then this spring is either rusted or broken. Wear on the cogwheels or the chain itself is almost unknown with this type of regulator, as the chains are of the usual type used on bicycles, and the amount of use they get in a window regulator is negligible.

However, it sometimes happens that if the regulator has not been used for years, as may be the case on rear doors or even front passenger doors, the chain may have rusted up and gone very stiff. Usually you can get such a chain flexible again by soaking it in penetrating oil and by working the links backwards and forwards, but if it has rusted to the point where it refuses to become flexible, you

Left **Washing in a mixture of paraffin and oil will usually make a seized chain flexible again. If not, try your local cycle shop for a replacement**

Below **If the chain you get is too long, you can shorten it with a link extractor, also from your local cycle shop**

should have no difficulty in replacing it with a length of chain from the cycle shop, and by joining the ends with the usual type of connector link. There are two standard widths of chain for cycles, so it pays to take the old chain with you when you need to buy a new one. The chain you buy will probably be far too long but the cycle shop will also sell you a link extractor, so that you can shorten it quite easily. Shortening a chain by trying to file off the ends of the hard rivets is a finger-aching and time-consuming job, whereas the extractor, which costs very little, will do the job in a few moments.

# Index